INCREASING RESTAURANT SALES

Boost Your Sales & Profits By Selling More Appetizers, Desserts, & Side Items

By B.J.Granberg

The Food Service Professional's Guide To:
Increasing Restaurant Sales Boost Your Sales &
Profits By Selling More Appetizers, Desserts, & Side
Items: 365 Secrets Revealed

Atlantic Publishing Group, Inc. Copyright © 2003
1210 SW 23rd Place
Ocala, Florida 34474
800-541-1336
352-622-5836 - Fax

www.atlantic-pub.com - Web Site
sales@atlantic-pub.com - E-mail

SAN Number :268-1250

International Standard Book Number: 0-910627-25-8

Library of Congress Cataloging-in-Publication Data

Granberg, B. J., 1944-
Increasing restaurant sales: boost your sales & profits by
selling more appetizers, desserts, & side items : 365 secrets
revealed / by B.J. Granberg.
p. cm. -- (The food service professionals guide to)
ISBN 0-910627-25-8 (paper : alk. paper)
1. Restaurants--Marketing. 2. Food service management.
3. Appetizers. 4. Desserts. 5. Side dishes (Cookery)   I.
Title.II. Series.
TX911.3.M3G72 2003
647.95'068'8--dc21
 2002013543

Printed in Canada

Book layout and design by Meg Buchner of Megadesign
www.mega-designs.com • e-mail: megadesn@mhtc.net

CONTENTS

INTRODUCTION

Whether your restaurant is a mom and pop operation with paper napkins and plastic utensils or a gourmet, fine-dining establishment, with white linen table cloths, candlelight and polished silverware, you can increase sales and launch a great reputation by featuring "can't pass up" menu sub-items such as appetizers and desserts.

For example, if your restaurant specializes in fried chicken, that's more than likely what your clientele will be hungry for when they walk in the door. They probably won't have given much thought to the delicious skins-on mashed potatoes or fresh green beans - or even the homemade peach cobbler topped with a scoop of vanilla bean ice cream.

But, never underestimate the power these items have to make your customers' experience at your restaurant a memorable one. Promoting side items on your menu can be a money-making venture for you. It will help you establish a reputation that will spread word-of-mouth and keep your customers returning on a regular basis. Side items on any restaurant's menu can bring in more profit for you - more tips for your waitstaff and more satisfaction for your customers if you know which side items to feature and how to sell them.

"Increasing Your Restaurant Sales By Selling More Appetizers, Desserts, Side Items And Beverages: 365 Secrets Revealed" will show you how to use side items such as desserts, appetizers and beverages to increase sales and profits – what works and what doesn't – and how to keep your customers coming back for more!

The key to building restaurant sales is to increase volume from your existing customer base.

CHAPTER ONE

MAKING $$$ FROM
SUPER SUB-MENU ITEMS

Customers for Life and a Word of Caution

Take care of your guests, and your sales will take care of themselves. "Customers for life" means that once guests come to your restaurant, they'll never be satisfied with your competitors. Simple, right? It also means that the real work of building sales doesn't happen with your advertising schedule or marketing plan, but on the floor, with your customers.

The key to building restaurant sales is to increase volume from your existing customer base. Think about it: If your customers were to return just one more time per month, that would be an increase in sales volume of between 15 and 50 percent! These are people who already know about you, live within an acceptable travel distance and will recommend you to their friends if you make them happy. These are the people you want to target in order to build a regular, loyal customer base that shares the pleasures of your establishment with friends.

So how do you do this? Work on building loyalty, not necessarily the check average! Don't get too wrapped up in increasing the check average to the point guests feel they are being "sold."

It's true: A bigger check is a bigger sale. However, selling techniques designed to boost check averages can be dangerous if customers feel they are being pressured. Guests come first. Your income comes from serving people, not food. Focusing only on the bottom line or a higher check average puts your customers second at best. If everyone who ever ate at your restaurant were so pleased that he couldn't wait to come back with their friends, what would your sales be like? If eating with you didn't thrill your customers, if they felt pressured to order something expensive or a dessert they really did not want, what difference would it make how big their check was when they won't be coming back?

Suggestive selling can work and work well to the delight of your guests. If it's done well it can be very effective. The problem is it needs to be done well. Don't run the risk of your guests thinking they come in a distant second to their money. The safest way to achieve sales growth is to have your guests return more often. Focusing on this is a win-win situation. Your goal is to delight them, win their loyalty and put them first, first, first! If you're a restaurant patron – and you are – what will have you coming back for another meal: your waiter focusing on getting you to spend more money or on treating you like royalty? This is a fine line that must be constantly reinforced to your waitstaff.

Know What Your Patrons Want

The type of restaurant that you manage naturally dictates the types of side items that will appeal to your customers. For example, an escargot appetizer plate probably wouldn't appeal to your clients if you operate a family-style restaurant that features chicken-fried steak with mashed potatoes and gravy. But, how do you figure out what your patrons want to see on the menu? Here's how:

- **Experiment with your menu.** Discover what works (and what doesn't) by doing a monthly sales tally of every side item on your menu. This will help weed out the items that aren't being recognized and boost even more sales of the most popular menu items. Highlight the "winning" items on your menu and advertise them, wherever you can.

- **Learn from trends.** Always check out restaurant reviews in your local newspapers and magazines. Keep up to date on what's hot in restaurants across the country. Web sites such as www.martinsnet.com/restaurantlinks.asp are great sources of information about what's happening in the restaurant business.

- **Make them feel special.** Whenever you get a slower time, have a server take a cart around with a sampling of a new dish you're considering serving. Ask patrons to give their opinions on the items. They'll appreciate the consideration – and the freebie!

- **Stimulate the appetite with sub-menu items.** Use glowing adjectives to describe side items. For example, "Our Cokes are served in ice-cold frosty mugs." Place "menu tents" with colorful photos of your featured desserts on the table. These methods are sure to get your sub-menu items noticed. You can order table tents from www.armsco.com in a variety of styles – from acrylic to leather!

- **Advertise your specialty items.** Advertise (without spending a dime) with tactics like placing items such as desserts in a showcase, at the entrance of your restaurant. You can have exact replicas made of your dishes from www.trengovestudios.com so that you don't have to keep changing and wasting real food in the display case! Menu tents featuring a wide array of side items are also great advertising tools.

- **The best advertising comes from your waitstaff.** Be sure they're trained to properly present side items.

- **Offer beverages to whet the appetite.** Tell your customers about any "specials" on drinks – and don't make them wait too long once they've placed the drink order. Waiting will frustrate your clients and they'll be more apt to move quickly on to the entrée rather than ordering an appetizer.

- **Know the side items on your menu.** Don't take it for granted that a customer will know what "Loco Peñas" are. Even if a description appears on the menu with the item, be sure that your waitstaff knows its ingredients and how it's prepared.

- **Regionalize your menu.** Which side items are popular in your region? For example, extra-spicy side items might be more popular if you're in Texas or New Mexico, whereas if you're located in Maine, Clam Chowder is more likely to be a winner. Before you plan your menu, know what's popular in your region. You can find tips on regional food advice at www.eatethnic.com.

- **Offer seconds and freebies.** Offering "seconds" on mashed potatoes or bread won't noticeably decrease your profits, but it will go a long way toward promoting good will. A free dessert to a birthday celebrant makes a dining experience memorable. A free appetizer with a specialty drink order is yet another way to encourage your customers to return time and again.

- **Sell wine to win.** Selling more wine can send your profits soaring and make your waitstaff happy by the tips that come with it. If you decide to sell wine, be sure to be knowledgeable. Books such as *Windows on the World Complete Wine Course* (available at Barnes and Noble) by Kevin Zraly and Peter Sichel or *The Wine Bible* (available at Amazon) by Karen MacNeil, can increase your knowledge of wines. You might also check in to wine-appreciation courses at your community college.

- **Make friends with your suppliers.** Your vendors can help you select and market side items that will be hits with your customers. They'll benefit from your increased sales too! Vendors are aware of what's hot in other restaurants and can help you with promotions by providing free sales tools such as menu tents.

- **Using side items to create memorable moments.** Instruct your waitstaff to make a memorable experience of their customers' dining experience. Ask them if they're celebrating a special occasion – or perhaps this is their first time at your place. Offer them a free appetizer, drink or dessert to commemorate the occasion. They'll be back!

- **Don't just sell – appeal to your customers.** You won't need to "hard sell" customers to buy appetizers, drinks and desserts if you work beforehand to make those items appealing. Colorful menus, menu tents, displays and a waitstaff willing to make suggestions are excellent ways to "soft sell" your customers into buying more than just an entrée.

Include Your Waitstaff In Sub-Menu Item Decisions

Ask your waitstaff what works and what doesn't. It stands to reason that your waitstaff will know more about what pleases the customers and what doesn't. Ask for their input. If they know that you take their advice seriously, they'll pay closer attention to customers' feedback. The following tips will help you get your staff involved:

- **Make selling side items worth their while.** Promote the side items that will fatten the tab and make it more worth the waitstaffs' efforts by increasing the money in their pockets – and let them know what you're doing!

- **Have a contest.** Award a prize to the server who sells the most menu side items each month. It doesn't have to be an expensive prize; a lottery ticket or a special button to wear showing your appreciation are great recognition prizes. You can even give them an old-fashioned trophy engraved with their name! Order them online for a low price at www.quicktrophy.com.

- **Keep your waitstaff informed about new side items.** Be sure to post any changes in your menu and also changes to ingredients or preparation of a side item. This tactic will avoid embarrassing your waitstaff. It will also avoid frustration on the part of your customers if an item isn't prepared as the menu states or the waitstaff fails to mention a "new" item.

- **Include your greeters in promoting sub-menu items.** Your greeters can be a valuable part of your team if you include them in the selling process.

They can always start the "thinking" process by suggesting beverages, appetizers, a special side dish or even desserts before the guests are seated.

- **Show your waitstaff the difference between a sample ticket that includes side items and resulting tips** – and one that doesn't. Nothing is as motivating as money – and once your waitstaff sees the different that side items play in increasing tips, they'll be more inclined to suggest them to their customers.

- **Encourage your waitstaff to make suggestions.** Have regular meetings with your waitstaff and be sure to compliment them (or maybe reward them) on any side item suggestions that become a success on your menu.

- **Create a "pretend" ticket where the customer ordered a beverage and an entrée.** Then, create another ticket where the customer ordered an appetizer before dinner, traded up from a glass of beer to a pitcher and also ordered dessert and after-dinner drinks. Point out the difference to your staff. Don't forget to include an average tip in both cases.

- **Get their attention!** Motivate your waitstaff to recommend side items to their customers by grabbing their attention first. Money, recognition and praise work! Set goals for them and then reward them when they reach those goals. Be sure that you praise them in front of other waitstaff too.

- **Schedule "kitchen" sessions to get your servers involved.** The more your waitstaff knows about the ingredients in your menu items, the better their sales will be. Let them taste, cook and make suggestions for new and tried-and-true items. Your servers should always know how a dish is prepared and what ingredients are involved. You might also want to offer a written manual and a kitchen notebook so that they can take notes. Always be open to their suggestions.

- **Offer continuous training.** A stellar training program for your waitstaff will not only increase their knowledge so that they can perform better, it will also attract a much higher caliber of waitstaff to your restaurant. A well-trained group of servers will feel more a part of the operation and offer suggestions more freely. Keep in mind that your waitstaff is your most valuable asset in running a restaurant business.

- **Know your appetizers!** Be sure that your waitstaff (and greeters) have tasted the appetizers on your menu and that they're aware of any changes or specials. You can present new (or changed) appetizers in your weekly sales meetings and ask for your waitstaffs' opinions. It's a great way to get your employees thinking "appetizers," and they'll be able to make personal recommendations to their guests.

Place Side Items on a Pedestal

Don't forget the side items in your quest to sell more entrées. Side items can increase your profit margin even more than a high-priced entrée. Don't disregard them in your menu-planning process. Plan promotions and displays that will appeal to your clientele. Consider the following possibilities:

- **Regale your sub-menu items to reap profits.** You can give your sub-menu items a special place on your menu by directing your waitstaff to promote them, or by setting up displays that are inviting and colorful. Promotions that feature special side items such as a mid-winter "Evening in the Tropics" served with Jamaican Rum Punch or Mango Sundaes can get your customers out of the winter doldrums!

- **If you have a "Happy Hour," be sure to offer samples of appetizers.** "Happy Hour" customers can also be "return" lunch or dinner customers. They'll remember a delicious appetizer they sampled at "Happy Hour" and recommend it to their friends. "Happy Hour" can be an excellent promotional tool if you make it a memorable experience for your customers.

- **Don't forget the art of presentation.** No matter how delicious your sub-menu items are, presenta-tion is the key to really get them noticed. Garnishes, waitstaff knowledge and displays are all part of the art of presenting your side items.

- **If you sell wine, "put it on a pedestal."** There's a definite art to presenting wine that will increase your sales. See section 4, "Bottoms Up – How to

Increase Beverage Sales" for more information on presenting wines and other beverages.

- **"Scratch and sniff" your menu items!** You can add scratch and sniff stickers to certain parts of your menu or table tents to attract patrons to the delectable smells of the ingredients you'll be using. Order yours from Mello Smello at 800-328-4876, www.mellosmello.com.

- **Be sure your glassware, dishes and utensils are spotless.** Ask your waitstaff to help you keep tabs on the condition of serving items. Nothing turns a customer off from dining at your restaurant more than spots (or even worse – lipstick!) on glasses or crusty food left on a fork. Don't let it happen!

- **Offer something different.** When you offer a side item that is different from the usual fare, your guests will perceive it as a good value. A vivid description of the item also plays a big role in turning a customer's head. For example, rather than offering a "baked potato with a steak," offer a "ramekin of Julienne potatoes, prepared with real butter and a special blend of four types of cheeses."

- **Make side items stand out on your menus.** Use color and a larger typeface to make side items "stars" on your menus. If they're buried in small type or an obscure corner, they may never have a chance to increase sales for your business.

- **Offer free side items when you advertise.** Coupons for free side items, such as beverage or appetizers, are a sure-fire way to increase traffic in your restaurant. You can order flyers from

www.kinkos.com. Have a staffer place them on the
windshields of cars near your establishment!

- **Serve up some collectibles with your sides.** If
  it's Christmas season, you can serve one new
  collectible each week including Santa, Frosty the
  Snowman, Rudolph and an angel. They can be an
  individual part of the presentation, or something
  that actually holds a serving of a particular side
  item. Patrons will keep coming back week after
  week to get the entire set!

- **Serve your side items with flourish.** Don't bury
  side items on a plate overpowered by an entrée.
  Serve them in special dishes or glassware and use
  garnishes and color to further highlight them. You
  can order reasonably priced party dishware at
  www.fiesta-dinnerware.com.

- **Offer free side dishes with the purchase of a
  major item, such as a bottle of wine.** Consider
  promotion combinations such as offering a free
  appetizer with the purchase of a bottle of wine or a
  free dessert when they order the evening special.
  Not only will this promotion increase goodwill and
  sales revenue, but it will also encourage your
  customers to try something different.

- **Increase your lunch crowd business by running
  specials on side items.** Typical lunch clientele is
  usually looking for good food and fast service. You
  can capitalize on the situation by featuring quickly
  prepared side items, such as appetizers, while
  they're waiting on entrées or offering a "to-go" box
  with a dessert.

- **Appeal to kids when displaying side items.** If you

run a family-style restaurant, get the kids in on the side item sales. For example, you could offer a handout with a creative drawing of a side item special. Provide crayons and they'll be busy coloring the item while their order is being prepared!

Preparation and Presentation of Side Items Promote Sales

Dare to be different in your food fare's preparation. Try a few of the following novel suggestions for enhancing your presentation of side items:

- **Prepare routine fare in an unusual way.** Even a plain potato can be prepared differently than the usual ways of mashing or baking. Grill them with some liquid smoke sprinkled on top, or batter chicken fingers with a Cajun-spiced mixture for extra zing.

- **Enthusiastic descriptions.** Be sure your customers know that you've put a great deal of effort into being different. For example, how about the following description for the preparation of your potatoes: "Our smoky, grilled potatoes have a hickory flavor that complements our grilled hamburgers."

- **Side item aromas can whet your customers' appetites.** Fresh herbs produce aromas that will appeal to your customers' sense of smell. Basil, tarragon and rosemary are herbs that can be used in many side items to produce delicate, appealing scents. Fresh-baked bread is also a winner in the aroma department.

- **Prepare side items that will please your customers' palates.** Marinating ingredients is a wonderful way to make the ordinary dish stand out. For example, try soaking fresh vegetables in a flavorful marinade or experiment with layering flavors within the same dish, for example, grilled chicken fingers with a tomato-cream sauce topped with Bleu Cheese.

- **Flame the fires!** If someone orders Bananas Foster or fajitas for their meal or dessert, then try to serve the dish while it's still on fire or sizzling. The special effect will bring attention to the order and increase sales.

- **Water has a calming effect.** If you're serving a beautiful side dish with edible flowers, you might consider bringing out a clear serving platter that showcases some water on the bottom and gives the effect of floating fare.

- **Use various cheeses as appetizers or to complement a main dish.** America is sold on cheese. With today's wide varieties of taste and color, you can create cheese appetizers that will appeal to your customers' sense of nutrition and taste. Try using cheeses as toppings on side dishes and desserts. You can learn all about the various uses of cheese at www.cheese.com.

- **Attractively displayed fruit can complement any meal.** Don't forget to add fruit to a plate as a garnish. Its colorful appeal is a great alternative to parsley. Try something different. Rather than grapes, garnish a plate with a thin watermelon slice, an orange wedge or a small bunch of cherries. And don't just cut it the standard, boring way – make it pretty!

- **Specialty cutlery.** Order some specialty cutlery at www.cooking.com.

- **Use oversized dishware.** Plates, cups and platters will have an appealing effect on the presentation of your fare, so try to giant-size the platters, not necessarily the portions.

- **Give bread the attention it deserves.** Bread served with a meal is very important to most diners. There is a trend toward unusual breads such as caraway rye or Irish soda bread. Bread sticks are popular side items too and can be served topped with garlic spreads or herbs. Good and unusual breads will impress your customers and is a very economical side item choice. You can find out all sorts of fun bread facts and learn the secrets to baking the best of breads at www.breaddaily.tripod.com.

- **Build a tortilla factory.** If your restaurant serves Mexican or Tex-Mex meals, you might invest in a see-through kitchen that allows patrons to watch the tortilla-making process right from the comfort of their tables! Give your guests a visual experience!

- **Serve your customers colorful and tasty spreads as a break from butter or margarine.** A strawberry-butter blend for pancakes or an herbed butter for bread is an especially good accompaniment that will appeal to your customers. It's a very simple and low-cost method to set your restaurant apart from the others.

- **Have the chef make an impression.** If you're serving a large portion of a rare, expensive meat appetizer, have the chef come to the table to "prepare" the special in front of the customer.

Secret Specials to Showcase Your Sides

Here are some extra tips for "showcasing" your sides:

- **Place your side dishes on center stage.** Grits in the South – blended with cheese, shrimp or Cajun spices – take center stage. Special fruits – prepared grilled or honey basted – are Hawaii's top side dishes. Experiment with side dishes and find new, appealing ways to serve them.

- **Clue your patrons in on a little secret.** If you have a superb peach cobbler made out of fresh peaches that sells out night after night, have your servers clue patrons in to that fact right when they place their entrée orders. That way, customers are guaranteed a wonderful dessert and you're guaranteed a dessert sale!

- **Make reservations – for fabulous fare!** If some of your meals are rarities where there may not be enough to go around for an entire client base, offer reservations for certain entrées. Customers can call ahead and order their share of freshly imported Mahi-Mahi or another hard-to-get item.

- **Consider table-side preparation of side items.** Caesar salads are popular at restaurants that prepare them table-side. Many side items are easily prepared at the table on a pushcart – and will entertain and delight your guests at other tables as well.

- **Sell all-you-can-eat soup specials.** Whenever you serve a meal that is prefaced with a soup or salad, consider offering seconds, thirds or a larger portion of the soup to your patrons. You don't have to do it for soup-only buying customers, but when combined with a meal, as a starter dish, it turns out to be a very economical way of tempting guests.

- **Use "combination specials" to sell more appetizers.** You can combine appetizers with beverage sales and offer them at a reduced price to increase sales and get your customers to try new items on your menu. For example, you might try a glass of wine and appetizer combination at a reduced price. Be sure that your waitstaff knows about the specials you're offering and that they suggest them immediately to your guests.

CHAPTER TWO

TRAINING GREETERS AND WAITSTAFF TO PROMOTE SIDE ITEMS

The Art of Suggesting Accompaniments

Well-trained waitstaff are one of the most important tools you can utilize to promote side items on your menu. You can even train greeters to make suggestions that will make your customers aware of specials before they're seated. When your greeters and waitstaff realize how promoting side items can also magnify their gratuities, they'll be eager to learn how! Training your staff in the art of suggestion is an investment on which you can't afford to miss out! It can mean the difference between a successful operation that boasts of regular customers and the failure of a restaurant to communicate with its customers. Try the following approach:

- **Involve your staff.** As you're planning promotions for side items, let your waitstaff be a part of the exercise. The end result is that they'll feel more a part of the business and that will show in improved customer service and sales.

- **Increase tips by suggesting side items.** When your waitstaff convinces a customer to include a side item, such as dessert or an appetizer with their meal, the tips will increase right along with the total price of the meal.

- **Don't make your customers have to ask about specials or side items.** Make providing information an ingrained part of your waitstaffs' service. First, be sure they know about the items and then be sure they know how to suggest them. Most of all, encourage your waitstaff to be attentive and diligent about providing necessary information to customers.

- **Sell more beverages by suggesting that your customers "trade up."** For example, if a party of four orders four glasses of beer, suggest that a pitcher will cost less and provide an extra round. They'll appreciate the suggestion and might spend the "extra" money on an appetizer or dessert.

- **Have your servers point out menu tents that feature specialties or side items.** The best time to suggest most side items is when you first greet the customer and take their drink order. When you return to the table, you can say, "Have you had time to decide on an appetizer?" Also, have them verbally point out (and physically point to) the table tent, in case they haven't noticed it yet.

- **Suggest accompaniments at the appropriate times.** For example, when your customers order desserts, instruct your servers to suggest coffee or a wine that complements the dessert. A good time to suggest a side dish is when the server takes an entrée order, for instance, "Would you like to try our fresh, creamed asparagus with your filet mignon?"

- **If you happen to be sold out of an item that your customer requests, quickly suggest another item.** Never say you "ran out" of an item.

Instead, say you "sold out." Then, quickly suggest another item. True, there's not much difference between "ran out" and sold out," but the impact on your guests will be much more subtle.

- **Discuss with your waitstaff how to guide customers in their decision-making.** As a group, discuss items that your servers (and greeters) might suggest to customers. Also discuss ways to suggest those items to your guests. For example, a greeter can make a number of suggestions to your guests before they are seated. A discussion should be a great brainstorming session that will improve both tips and service.

- **Suggest items in pairs.** When suggesting a beer or cocktail, guide your customers toward an appetizer that would complement the drink. For example, "Our Gold Margaritas are on special today, and they really hit the spot with our stuffed jalapeño peppers."

- **Greeters can also suggest appetizer items.** Greeters can be excellent salespeople if they are taught to make suggestions, even before the guests are seated or immediately after. Have them recommend at least two appetizers or mention any specialties you might have. For example, "Be sure to consider our Cajun-spiced chicken wings for an appetizer. They're extremely popular here."

- **Be sure to suggest multiple appetizers to groups of four or more.** Groups of four or more present an excellent opportunity to suggest a variety of appetizers. Guests in groups usually want to relax and "graze" over drinks and food before actually ordering dinner. Take advantage of this situation: increase the tab and please your guests at the same time by making appetizer suggestions.

Know How to Serve Wine

If your restaurant serves wine, a certain amount of training and preparation will enhance your service and appeal to your customers – it will also help increase sales of this high profit margin item! Below are the basic steps to help your servers to sell more wine:

- **If a wine bucket is used, place it to the right** of the person who ordered the wine.

- **Present the bottle to the person who ordered the wine,** pointing out the vintage and name for the customer's approval.

- **When approved, proceed to serve.**

- **Cut the foil or plastic covering the cork, just below the second lip of the bottle.** Place the covering in your pocket, not on the table or in the wine bucket.

- **Insert the corkscrew at an angle** and turn until only one notch of the spiral is above the cork.

- **Tilt the corkscrew so that it is resting on the lip of the bottle** and hold in place with your forefinger.

- **Pull the corkscrew straight up,** being careful not to bend the cork.

- **Move cork gently from side to side,** while gently pulling from the bottle.

- **Untwist the corkscrew** from the cork and place the cork to the right of the host's glass.

- **Wipe the lip and mouth of the bottle** before pouring it for the host and then pour about a third of a portion (1 ounce).

- **When the host approves the wine, begin pouring for others at the table.**

- **Always replace wine glasses if they become smudged** or contain sediment. To learn even more about the art of serving wine to your guests, visit www.ichef.com/winecellar.

Timing is Everything

From the moment your guests enter your restaurant, timing is essential. Consider the following important timing factors:

- **Seating guests.** Inevitably, occasionally, your guests may have to wait to be seated or to be served. Be honest about the wait, and offer them a complimentary drink or an appetizer before their meal.

- **Serving your customers promptly will help you sell more appetizers.** The very best time to suggest an appetizer is when you take the beverage order. Point out a couple of appetizers that go with the beverages that they order. For example, beer-battered and fried cheese sticks with marinara dip might be suggested when your guests order a pitcher of beer. When you return with the beverages, don't forget the appetizers. You might say, "Have you decided which appetizer you want with your beer tonight?"

- **If your waitstaff concentrates on service, side item sales (and resulting tips) will follow.** Quick and efficient service when delivering your guests' first drink of the evening will go a long way when a waiter then suggests an appetizer or side dish. Don't provide expected service to your guests; go the extra mile and provide exemplary service.

- **Don't bring your customers' entrées until they're finished with the appetizers.** It is extremely important to monitor your guests' progress and to time delivery of the next item accordingly. If you bring an entrée before they're finished with the appetizer or a dessert before they've eaten the entrée, your customers will feel rushed and their dining experience at your restaurant may be ruined.

- **Bring another basket of bread before taking the empty one.** Bread is an important accompaniment to your guests' meal. Rather than take an empty bread basket away and leave them with nothing, bring a full basket and then remove the empty one.

- **Don't let your guests sit with a cold cup of coffee.** Again, monitoring your guests' progress to better time refills or fresh cups of coffee will assure the guests of a hot, fresh cup of coffee and that you're watching out for their needs. The waitstaff will benefit by this gesture with increased tips.

- **Before your customers leave your restaurant, thank them for coming.** Don't let your guests leave without first asking if they enjoyed the food and service. And don't forget to invite them back.

- **If there is a shift change while your guests are dining, don't let them wait** for continuing service. It is appropriate to have the new server introduce himself or herself and be aware of where the customer is (first drinks, entrée, etc.) with their meal.

- **Know how to time food orders for pickup.** Effective servers know how to work with the kitchen staff so that orders don't sit on a counter and wilt or become cold. Encourage your waitstaff to pay attention to this procedure to better serve their customers.

- **Don't present the check too early – or too late.** A check presented to the guest before he or she has even looked at the dessert menu rushes the customer and loses a chance for the waitstaff to earn more tips. If a check is presented too long after the dessert or the final order, the customer may become anxious or frustrated so that no matter how good the service was throughout the meal, your guests will leave with a negative attitude.

- **If you serve a buffet meal, be sure the waitstaff is well aware of when to replenish trays or bowls.** Don't make your customers have to stand and wait while a server returns to the kitchen for more buffet fare. Your guests' other food will cool off and the line will be held up. Also, cater to the customers who arrive at the last moments of the buffet. The trays should be full until the buffet serving hours are completely over.

Reinforce Customers' Decisions and Focus on Their Needs

Reassuring your customers that they have made good choices is a tried-and-tested method of increasing sales. Here's how to reinforce customers' decisions – and significantly increase your profits:

- **Use the "yes" nod.** Nodding "yes" as you make suggestions is a proven psychological tool for enticing your customers to say "YES!" to your side-item offers.

- **Surprise compliments.** Nothing makes a better impression than to have the manager walk around and personally greet patrons while they're dining. A handshake and a thank you, and you've garnered a loyal guest! When you do this, make an effort to occasionally comp the party's round of drinks – it will make them feel as if they're really a guest, and not a paying customer.

- **Encourage your customers to try new items by complimenting their choices.** For example, even if what the customer has chosen isn't one of your favorites, you can still say something reassuring such as, "Great choice! That's a very popular item here."

- **Guide your customers on items they may not be sure of, and then remember to compliment them!** Choosing items, such as wine, may be confusing to your guests. Be sure you know enough about the items to guide your customers into making a good decision. You can learn how to help others choose the best wine at www.vtwines.com/choosewine.

- **Taste everything on the menu so that you can make personal recommendations.** Nothing reinforces your customers' decisions more than a personal recommendation from you. Tell them about side items that may not be as prominent on the menu, but ones that you think are "outstanding."

- **Don't just focus on making the tab larger;** please your customers and larger tips will follow. Always focus your attention on what your guests want and need. Guide them well in ordering items and you'll form a connection with them that will maximize your income.

- **Include service with a smile.** It's such a simple thing to do to increase sales and patronage, but in our busy world, we often forget to smile at our customers and fail to provide them with service that will keep them coming back. The winning combination of these two intangibles can set up your customers to feel more at ease. Also, they'll be more apt to order appetizers with their beverages or desserts after their meal.

- **If your customers have a problem with their food or drinks, quickly guide them to another choice.** Always handle problems quickly and efficiently. Remove the plate of food or beverage from the table and then return immediately to suggest ways (or another item) that might solve the problem. Never argue with their opinion; just apologize and try to remedy the situation.

- **Listen to your customers.** No cheese on those cheese fries? No problem! Want your appetizer left un-breaded? Fine by us! Make sure people know when they come to you, you'll pay attention to their preferences.

- **Managers can promote good public relations.** A good manager will wander around the restaurant, chatting with customers and asking about the quality of the meal they've been served. This is also a good time to find out how a new item is being received by your diners.

- **Encourage your waitstaff to recognize regular customers.** Massage your regular customers' egos by training your waitstaff to remember and recognize return customers to your restaurant. Have them suggest a new appetizer to go with their "usual" beverage or remember something they mentioned last time they were in, such as "How are you liking that new job, Ms. Jones?"

- **Make your house customers feel special.** If your bar customers are ordering house wine, don't make them feel any less special by bringing a wine glass already filled to the table. Instead, bring the bottle to the table, and serve it just as you would if they had splurged on one of the expensive bottles!

- **Observe your guests before they order and after they've had a chance to sample the items.** Anticipate your guests' needs, such as approaching a newly seated table and saying, "Can I get you a drink from the bar? Perhaps some coffee or tea?" Also, notice the look on your customers' faces as they take their first bite of an item. If a mistake has been made, or if there is a problem with the food, addressing the problem quickly can avoid even more problems.

- **Don't offer larger portions.** Instead, offer free seconds. People will appreciate getting something for nothing in that form, better than if they were served a bigger portion initially.

- **Offer a formal invitation.** Depending on the setting of your restaurant, you might be able to have your waitstaff deliver formal invitations to patrons that read, "You are hereby invited by your waiter to join us for a coffee in the reserved room for after-dinner guests."

- **Thank-you cards are always in good taste.** There are several ways you can opt to issue "thank yous" to your patrons. You could ask your reservations to give their full mailing information, and then mail thank-you cards for every kept reservation. Or, if that idea is too much, you could send thank-you cards to groups who hold their meetings at your place!

Incentives to Sell

Money isn't the only incentive for selling side items. Believe it or not, increasing the total dollar value on the tab isn't the only reason that you should be selling side items. By pleasing your customers when you suggest a side item that complements their meal – or by actually saving them money by suggesting a pitcher rather than a glass of beer – you will foster customer loyalty and increase your servers' tips each time they return to your restaurant. Motivate your staff by offering them incentives:

- **Provide your waitstaff with incentives to sell side items.** Contests, recognition and rewards are all ways to help your staff realize that selling more menu side items can be worth their while.

- **Offer educational opportunities to your waitstaff.** Almost everyone appreciates the opportunity to better themselves in a chosen field or endeavor. Your waitstaff is no exception. There are many courses, training manuals and videos out there that will encourage your waitstaff to gain proficiency in things like how to sell more beverages, appetizers and desserts. Atlantic Publishing produces many of these educational aids. You can reach them at 800-541-1336 or visit their Web site at www.atlantic-pub.com. These types of educational opportunities will not only increase sales, but also promote loyalty amongst your waitstaff.

- **Pride is an important incentive in selling anything.** Taking pride in how you perform on the job is an important mental reward. You can help this process along by praising exceptional waitstaff – especially in front of others. Rewards for jobs well done can also invoke a sense of pride in your waitstaff. Be sure that you address these issues in regular meetings with your staff.

- **Have a "company appreciation" week or month.** Let your servers know that for every new company they recruit for company appreciation week, they'll get a bonus! All you need is to get your foot in the door with the staff of nearby businesses and you'll find them coming back again and again!

CHAPTER THREE

APPETIZER SAVVY

Appetizers – Tantalizers!

Almost every country and culture enjoys some type of appetizer before the main course of a meal. Americans no longer think of appetizers as a salad, cocktail sausages or cheese and crackers. Stuffed jalapeño peppers, kabobs, spinach dips and chicken wings have all entered the appetizer market, making "appetizer savvy" a huge money-maker in restaurant sales. Appetizers are meant to whet the appetite of your customers and get them ready to enjoy the main course – the entrée. Appetizers also serve as "tantalizers" before the main meal to help your guests relax with an accompanying cocktail, glass of wine or other beverage of choice. The following ideas will increase your "appetizer savvy" and increase sales and profit – besides adding more tips for your waitstaff:

- **The "eyes" have it!** Eye appeal of prepared food is 90 percent of the reason people try a new or different dish. Be sure that your side items are presented with "eye appeal" in mind – on the dish, pictured on the menu, or described by your waitstaff.

- **Add flare to a meal with appetizers.** Appetizers can always add a distinctive flare to any restaurant's menu items. If you concentrate on serving appetizers with a flare, your sales will increase tenfold. This means using garnishes to add color and spices to add zest. Make them look just as the name suggests – appetizing!

- **Tantalize your guests with vivid descriptions.** For example, rather than say, "Would you like dessert?" say instead, "How about a piece of our luscious cherry cream pie? It's made with fresh cherries and lots of whipped cream on top!"

- **Use catchy names for your appetizer menu items.** It's great to serve delicious, one-of-a-kind nachos at your restaurant, but rather than listing them on the menu as "nachos," a name like, "Jamaican Jerk Nachos" will paint a picture in your customer's mind of something special. Imply that these nachos are not the type of regular, run-of-the-mill nachos, served at other restaurants. Your customers might ask you about them and you can then come up with a plethora of adjectives to convince them that this is the appetizer they should order.

- **Specialty drinks or specially-priced drinks.** Be sure that each shift of your waitstaff is aware of any specials on drinks that might not be on your menu. A customer will be more willing to try a new drink if it's presented first and sounds tantalizing.

- **Take an appetizer tour (around the world).** One way to sell more appetizers is to think of catchy promotions to highlight them and put them foremost in your customers' minds. A great promotion for appetizers might be to feature appetizers "around the world." You may want to do this on a continuing basis or to feature a specialty appetizer each week. For example, you might highlight "Greek Dolmades" (grape leaves stuffed with rice, pine nuts and special seasonings) one week and "Turkish Kabobs" another week.

- **Rethink the positioning of appetizers on your menu to make them more tantalizing.** Think about the role that appetizers serve in your restaurant niche. If they're extremely popular and a great source of sales revenue, you may want to increase their visibility on the menu. If you're thinking about making appetizers more a part of your sales, be sure to consider making them a very important and special part of your menu. Use color and flare to make them appetizing!

Kids Want Appetizers Too!

Kids are very influential in choosing which restaurant. In a recent poll, 55 percent of adults said that their kids were influential in choosing a place to dine. If you plan to make your restaurant "kid friendly," your menu must reflect this influence. Kids see their parents or siblings order appetizers and it's natural that they should want one too. Sometimes parents order appetizers in place of an entire meal for their children. If your restaurant caters to kids, families in this busy world will keep returning. Here are some tips to encourage sales of appetizers to kids:

- **Use sub-menu items to appeal to kids.** Kids will remember where they got those French fries in the shape of dinosaurs or the sundae named "Frosty the Snowman." Chances are, they'll plead to their parents for a return visit.

- **Consider a free baby-sitting service** while

parents dine. Many establishments realize that in today's world, families are spread out across the country and many often don't have a reliable network of friends that they can rely on to watch the kids while mom and dad go out for a relaxing evening. Reserve a special area of your restaurant for baby-sitting services. The kids will love playing instead of having to sit still and keep quiet at the dinner table.

- **Offer appetizers that will appeal to kids.** Mini-sized "Pigs in a Blanket" with Ranch dressing dip, featuring bites of sausages wrapped in bread and baked until golden brown is an excellent kids' appetizer. Ask your chef to come up with appetizers that will be visually appealing to kids as well as tasty.

- **Offer specials that will appeal to parents as well as kids.** Offering specials on children's appetizers will appeal to parents and kids alike. For example, you could offer a special of a kid's beverage paired with cheese sticks and dip at a reduced price.

- **Serve kids' appetizers in unusual containers,** or offer "prizes" with an appetizer order. We all know how McDonald's has profited by their Happy Meal featuring a toy in each bag. Offering kids, dining at your restaurant, a balloon when they leave or a "keeper" cup for their beverage are ways to make kids feel special and to keep them returning to your restaurant.

- **Offer some healthy appetizers on your kids' menu.** When parents take their children out to eat, they are often looking for a restaurant that features items that are healthy as well as tasty.

Appetizers such as mixed fruit salad or mini pizzas featuring toppings such as veggies are great items to have on the menu if parents are looking for a variety of healthy eating choices.

- **Use a mascot outdoors to bring in diners.** Having a staff member stand on the street corner acting goofy to draw attention to your restaurant sounds like a funny idea, but it works! Even better: have him or her carry a funny sign to go along with the costume!

- **Lend a hand to mom and dad.** If you see that the kids are enjoying your grilled eggplant appetizer, have a recipe card on hand to offer mom and dad as a way to get the young ones to eat more veggies!

- **Shape up or ship out.** If the fries and nuggets aren't unusually shaped, you might as well give up appealing to kids these days. McCain Foods, Inc., in Rosemont, Illinois, sells alphabet fries and dinosaur-shaped food items to get them intrigued.

- **Offer a mini menu.** Kids sometimes get the short end of the stick in today's restaurant industry. At most places, they get only two choices: chicken nuggets or a burger. Why not offer kids their choice of anything mom and dad are eating – only in a kids'-meal approach?

- **Let kids act as chefs.** If you've ever seen a Snackable, you'll understand why they're so popular with school-aged kids these days. Children love making things – even their own food! So why not order some miniature pizzas where you bring out the toppings and they lay it on thick before you pop it into the oven?

- **It's backwards tonight!** Kids love pancakes at night and burgers for breakfast. Why not have a special night of the week, when everything is backwards and you're serving up chocolate chip pancakes at 7:30 p.m. instead of a.m.?

- **Serve their teddy bears.** Many kids ask if they can bring their favorite toy inside the restaurant, but mom and dad usually have to say no. Why not make it okay to bring teddy along? They can sit in a special toy spot and even be served a couple of Teddy Graham crackers by the waitstaff!

- **Let the parents earn "Kids' Kash."** Every time your guests eat at your restaurant, they can earn a certain percentage of their bill in Kids' Kash. Have a printer print up some really funny fake money and then let the kids' cash in the moohlah for something like a toy from your treasure box or a daring dessert.

- **Older kids.** If there is a local youth sports program, find out if you can sponsor a team. After the big games, serve up free kids' meals to the boys and girls playing on your team, or bring appetizer-type foods to the game for them to grab on the go.

- **Set up a school incentive.** Teachers will be more than happy to give out free kids' meal certificates to those students who have achieved a certain goal for the month. Also, when they beg their parents to bring them in to collect on their accomplishment, you'll be serving to the rest of the family as well!

Appealing to the "Happy Hour" Crowd

Happy Hour is a great way to introduce your guests to new appetizers. If you feature a Happy Hour at your restaurant, consider offering appetizers free along with reduced prices on beverages. Here are some tips for promoting appetizers to the Happy Hour crowd:

- **Be contagious.** When your bar is enthusiastic, your patrons will be too! Have a rowdy good time, or serve up a relaxing scene – just make sure everyone is in sync when it comes to mood and ambiance during Happy Hour. Make sure servers are always in a positive frame of mind – it will rub off on your customers!

- **Hold Tuesday-night surprises.** Every Tuesday, between 5 and 7 p.m., have the greeting staff hand out random numbers to your patrons. Then, at 5:30, 6, and 7 p.m., have the bartender call out a random number. The winner gets a free appetizer that night! This will get people in for the appetizers and drink specials while they wait to see if they've won.

- **Know what your customers want when they come for Happy Hour.** A typical Happy Hour crowd is unwinding after a day at work. They want to relax and munch on something until it's time for dinner. Appetizers can enhance the taste of their drinks and will also keep the intoxication level down. Be sure to offer them to your Happy Hour guests.

- **Holi-daze your Happy Hour crowd.** If you have a room full of couples who came to the bar to celebrate their love on Valentines Day, why not offer up a platter full of heart-shaped appetizers? Perdue Farms in Salisbury, Maryland, sells heart-shaped chicken nuggets. Do the same for all holidays! Ornament-shaped meatballs, Christmas tree cookies. Be creative!

- **Back to the old days.** Offer the types of snack foods and candies that bring out the nostalgia in your guests. Why not stock the bowls full of fun items like wax lips or candy cigarettes in the smoking section? They'll reminisce at how they used to love those as a kid, and will then have fond memories of your place as well!

- **Don't skimp on your Happy Hour appetizers.** Many restaurants skimp on the appetizers they serve at Happy Hour and then wonder why they don't have more of a crowd. Offer a variety of appetizers and be sure they are presented in a colorful and tasteful manner. Also, make sure you don't run out.

- **Stick with finger foods at Happy Hour.** If you offer only finger foods at Happy Hour, you'll reduce cleanup (such as washing utensils) and present a more relaxed atmosphere for your customers. Be sure to offer plenty of napkins and plates, though.

- **Offer more and better Happy Hour food than your competition.** If you make your restaurant the place for Happy Hour gatherings, you'll reap the benefits in regular customers and word-of-mouth advertising that can't be beat. Many of your customers will probably be single men and women who may not want to cook dinner for only themselves. They are looking for a free "light" dinner after work with a cocktail or a glass of wine. If you make it worth their while to be there for Happy Hour, they'll become your regulars. Spend time, effort and money on your Happy Hour fare and you (and your customers) won't be disappointed.

• **Presentation of Happy Hour appetizers is very important.** Make your Happy Hour appetizers appealing to your customers. Use tablecloths, plant arrangements, garnishes and various elevations to make an appealing display.

• **Keep replenishing empty plates of food.** Nothing is worse than running out of food at Happy Hour. On the other hand, you must give a clear signal when Happy Hour is officially over. This can mean switching from one size glass to another or simply clearing away the munchies.

• **Offering appetizers at Happy Hour will increase your beverage sales.** Happy Hour isn't only a way to get your appetizers noticed. Serving appetizers will definitely increase your beverage sales. Many people will come for the free food, but chances are, they'll stay and order more drinks. Statistics show that when you serve appetizers at your Happy Hour, beverage sales increase up to 20 percent or more.

• **Use Happy Hour as an in-house opportunity to promote your appetizers.** Use table tents, chalk boards, flyers and other methods to advertise anything from more appetizers, side dishes, specialty beverages and lunch and dinner specials to catering or take-out dinners. The Happy Hour crowd is already in your restaurant because they enjoy being there. More than likely, they'll return for lunch or dinner!

- **Your Happy Hour appetizers don't have to be heavy or expensive.** Think of ways to keep the cost of your "free" appetizers down while keeping a delightful presentation. A combination of light and heavy appetizers will appeal to everyone. A great and inexpensive appetizer could be to take fresh loaves of French or Italian bread and fill them with meats and cheeses (be sure to have one with no meat for light eaters or vegetarians). Cut them into mini sandwiches and serve them with condiments.

- **Ask your waitstaff what is and isn't working for your Happy Hour.** Your waitstaff is an excellent source of information that you'll need to make your Happy Hour a success. They can let you know which appetizers customers are flocking to and which have no appeal. Be sure they know to promote other specials too, such as desserts, dinner specials, etc.

- **Free publicity is easy if you know how.** Happy Hour can be a great resource of fun, wacky contests. Use that time to come up with an off-the-wall idea to attract not only customers, but also the press to cover the event!

- **Write it on the table during Happy Hour.** If you can manage it, have the table covered in paper, with markers and crayons kept in a cup for patrons to doodle with while they eat. Whenever a waiter changes the paper, have him or her write a message touting a specific appetizer, such as, "Try our cheese-sticks!"

- **Beyond bar snacks.** There's no reason to subject your customers to beer nuts when they're waiting at the bar. Sam Malone, the main character in the sitcom "Cheers," learned that even loyal customers will go elsewhere if the Happy Hour appetizers are more appealing down the street.

Extra-Mile Appetizer Appeal

Stand out from the crowd – give your appetizers that extra "appeal"! Here's how:

• **Give the people choices!** People love it when they can order one item in a variety of ways. If you're serving a special appetizer, like a wonderful finger food, give the patrons their choice of three or four sauces to go with it!

• **Organic-lovers delight.** If you serve fresh vegetables as appetizers, why not offer patrons special organic ones as well? They'll love the fact that their edibles aren't contaminated with insecticide or pest repellents.

• **Appetizers appropriate for the diner.** If a single diner comes in to eat, it's obvious that he or she won't need as many items as a group of six or more. Why not offer different-sized appetizers? For one, two, or five or more!

• **Finger foods?** Finger bowls! If your appetizers are finger foods that might wind up making a mess, why not go the extra mile and have the server bring a few warm rolled washcloths with a small bowl of warm water and lemon?

• **Special utensils for special appetizers.** Skewers and toothpicks with confetti-looking tops always make an appetizer look more attractive.

- **Go hot or cold.** Cucumber soups are generally served cold, while potato soup is served hot. Find some variety of appetizers where patrons can choose how they want it served – chilly or tropical! Hint: You can do the same for desserts; some patrons may prefer hot fudge, while others prefer a dopple of cold fudge.

- **Serve up specialty butters.** Many restaurants now serve more than just the basic butter and margarine options. Today's consumers want special butters, like apple or blueberry butter! Find one pre-made ready to serve, or have your chef concoct one that reflects your signature style!

- **Toast your buns!** Homemade croutons go over very well if your establishment is one where appetizers rely heavily on salad mixtures. All you have to do is toast the bread, sauté it in a bit of flavored oil, and add seasoning.

- **Serve up signature spreads.** Jellies, jams and preserves are all extra special when you devise a way to make them unique to what's already out there. Experiment with seasonal berries until you find what works best for you and your patrons!

CHAPTER FOUR

"BOTTOMS UP" – HOW TO INCREASE BEVERAGE SALES

Promoting Beverages

If you follow a plan to increase beverage sales in your restaurant, you can be assured of increasing your profits, and tips for your waitstaff! From suggesting a bottle, rather than a glass of wine – or a pitcher rather than a glass of beer – when you excel at putting beverages on the tab, you'll excel at putting money in your pocket. You're in business to make money and if your guests aren't happy with their experience, they won't come back. Beverages and the service they require are a huge part of making sure that your clients leave refreshed and excited about your establishment. Focus on the following proven techniques for increasing your beverage sales:

- **Think media.** The media are always looking for new things to write about food service. Besides holiday events, try to think of new, creative angles about the beverages you serve that might just get a food service reporter excited enough to review and print! For example, you may have a new and exclusive selection of Greek wines and want to have a wine-tasting event. Couple that with appetizers from the region such as "Dolmades" or Hummus served with pita bread. Spend a little on decorations that capture the feel of the region and you have a "media event"! Send a press release to your local food editor and invite him or her in for the experience. You can get help crafting your own press release at www.press-release-writing.com, or have a professional write it for you for only $100 at www.writeconsultants.com.

- **Billboards or marquees can boost traffic in your business.** Using billboards can be as easy as parking your company car out in the parking lot by the street and writing on it with shoe polish. Or, you can use a marquee to attract customers and let them know your Cosmopolitans are $1 or top shelf liquors are half price.

- **Always suggest a "trade up" when it comes to beverages.** This is particularly effective for large groups of guests who are in "party mode" and likely to settle in for the evening. Be quick to recommend a "trade up"; perhaps bottles of wine rather than individual glasses, or pitchers of draft beer rather than served by the glass. Not only can this practice increase your sales, it can also let your customers know that you're interested in providing them with the most cost-effective way of purchasing their beverages.

- **Be known for something.** If you carry 130 different varieties of Scotch, then by all means, advertise it! Hang signs in the bar that say just that and make sure the local food editor gets wind of it too so that he or she can pass the word.

- **Advertise the fact that you have a comprehensive bar-food menu.** If you want to keep your customers at the bar, then you can develop a special menu that offers patrons a wider variety of bar fare than most of the other restaurants in town. For this, you'll be serving appetizer-like munchies at a larger portion.

- **You don't have to spend lots of money to promote beverages.** Attractive table tents, wine lists and chalkboard specials can be valuable props to promoting beverages. Always feature selections that your greeters and waitstaff can suggest as soon as the guests are seated. A number of suppliers can and will provide you, free of charge, with props that you can use to promote beverages in your restaurant. You can order them online at www.artedesigngroup.com.

- **Always offer your guests a choice when they're ordering wine or champagne.** If your guests haven't already ordered wine or champagne after you take their orders, take the opportunity to suggest one that would go with the food they ordered. Many people are shy when it comes to ordering a beverage to complement their order. A couple of suggestions on your part will help them to feel more confident with their choice.

- **Wine list.** Create an imaginative wine list with tasting notes to accompany each wine. Include a couple of unusual wines, such as the "new technology" Bordeaux reds. If you need more information about wine, its characteristics and grape varieties, visit www.demystifying-wine.com or www.grape-varieties.com.

- **Happy Hour is a great opportunity to promote beverages.** If you sponsor a Happy Hour at your establishment, you can use this time to offer a variety of specialty drinks that your dinner customers might not otherwise try. It's fun for your customers; it's also great advertising for you!

- **Don't forget to promote nonalcoholic drinks.**
  When you're thinking of promotions to sell wines,
  champagnes and specialty drinks, don't forget to
  include some nonalcoholic beverages. Coffee, tea
  and sodas can be a source of delight to your non-
  drinking guests, and kids too!

- **Kids' drinks can increase your beverage sales.** If
  your restaurant caters to families with kids,
  remember that kids absolutely love fun drinks that
  they can slurp through a straw, or one that comes
  in an unusual container.

- **After-dinner drinks present a great sales
  opportunity.** Many guests might order an after-
  dinner drink, such as an "Amaretto Coffee" instead
  of a dessert. Train your servers to know how to
  recommend an after-dinner drink and be sure they
  can make informative suggestions. These
  suggestions can result in a "double upsell" when
  your waitstaff can recommend desserts along with
  after-dinner drinks. For example, if a guest orders
  a simple bowl of fruit for dessert, your server
  might suggest a "topping" of Grand Marnier or
  Chambord.

- **Train your waitstaff to offer tempting
  appetizers with a guest's beverage order.** These
  two winners – appetizers and beverages – can be
  paired at a special price and used as a promotion
  to get your customers to try something different. It
  is also a good way to "off-load" slow movers or
  excess stock that is approaching its "sell-by" date.

- **Specials and promotions.** Don't simply depend on
  your servers to get the word out. Place colorful

table tents on tables or at every other bar stool to advertise drink and appetizer specials.

- **Have a forgetful promotion!** In many restaurants, you'll see the waitstaff wearing buttons that read, "FREE dessert if I forget to tell you about our daily specials." This will keep your servers on their toes and ensure the customers are listening attentively to the delicious spiel they're delivering! Order your custom-designed buttons at www.buttonstore.com.

- **Suggest trying something different from the "same-old" drink.** For example, your servers can suggest a Kir Royale rather than "only" a glass of champagne. It's a delectable drink made with champagne and a splash of crème de cassis. Blend the two and you have a sparkling, pink confection rather than "just" a glass of champagne.

- **Provide samples of a beverage if the customer isn't sure of what he or she wants.** Providing samples of beverages often encourage customers to buy additional drinks. Samples also make guests feel special and promote goodwill. An excellent time to offer sample drinks is when guests have to wait for a table or as soon as they're seated.

- **Call on your vendors to help you with beverage promotions.** Most suppliers are only too ready to help you promote the beverages they sell. They'll usually be pleased to help you create promotions that will bring in new customers and try their products. And besides, they have a much greater marketing allowance than you. Demand their assistance to help increase your business. Call on your vendors to be present at special sales meetings with your waitstaff. They can and will share valuable tips about their products to help your servers become confident in up-selling to their customers. It can only be a win-win situation for you and your suppliers.

Product Knowledge is Key to Boosting Beverage Sales

Before you can sell beverages for optimum profitability, it is vital that your staff is knowledgeable about the products they are selling. Consider the following ways to find out all about beverages and how to serve them:

- **Hold seminars or show videos to your waitstaff and greeters** on the proper ways to serve beverages such as wine. Wine is a proven bestseller. The more your waitstaff knows about how to serve them, the more sales your restaurant will realize. Atlantic Publishing, www.atlantic-pub.com, offers a variety of books, videotapes and software on sales tips for the hospitality industry.

- **Instruct your waitstaff as to which wines complement certain foods.** It doesn't make sense to have a wine cellar stocked with a wide variety of wines if your waitstaff doesn't know how to promote them. Time invested in teaching your staff the basics of wine will not only make your servers more money (as much as $2,500 a year or more!), but will put more money into your cash drawer. You may even get a bulk discount from your vendors! Be sure to visit sites such as www.geerwade.com for wine education and ideas.

- **Know your beverage labels.** Customers who know

their drinks are going to know the difference if you serve them a "margarita" instead of the "gold" margarita made with Cuervo Gold Tequila that they ordered. Teach your waitstaff to know drink labels and the difference in each. It will save you money in returned drinks and disgruntled customers. Also, if you want to find out more about wine labels, take a look at www.franklinmiamipublishing.com/wine.html.

- **Know what's in and what's out in beverage trends.** You'll be way ahead of the competition if you make it a point to find out current trends in the beverage industry. Beveragenet.net is a great Web site for newsy articles on beverage trends, including wines, cocktail recipes, coffee and tea or microbrews.

- **Know the ingredients.** Learning the ingredients contained in drinks is easy and can become a big selling tool for your waitstaff. If a customer asks for a Whiskey Sour and your server says, "Dewar's, Sir?" that customer will know he or she is being served by someone who knows the business. Most waiters know that "on the rocks" means that the customer wants his or her drink served over ice. But if the customer asks for a "mist," how many of your servers know that the drink should be served over crushed ice?

- **Train your servers in the unique way of presenting wine** and your sales will increase. Presenting a bottle of wine is unique, and if done properly, can impress your customers and most certainly add larger tips for your waitstaff. Some servers may not feel comfortable opening a bottle of wine. That's where special training pays off.

Have them practice until it becomes second nature to them. Perhaps you can let them open wines for your bartender to get some extra practice. Above all, be sure your waitstaff is equipped with wine openers and that you keep an extra supply on hand in case they forget or lose them. You can find techniques on the Web for opening wine at sites such as www.fontanacandida.com.

Imaginative Presentation Will Boost Beverage Profitability

Imaginative presentation can have a major impact on your beverage sales. Combine knowledge and presentation and you're on to a winner! Consider the following possibilities:

- **Feature wine by placing a bottle on the table.** By placing a bottle of wine on each table before the guests are seated, you are placing a seed in their minds to order it. The bottle also serves as a reminder to your waitstaff to tell them about the wine and if it's being offered at a special, reduced cost. This also encourages your guests to buy a bottle of wine rather than by the glass.

- **Use adjectives in your beverage presentations to sell more.** Use key words such as frosty, ice cold, piping hot and refreshing to entice your customers to buy more beverages. Rather than offering "just" coffee to a guest, try, "One of our famous iced-coffee drinks in a frosty glass would really taste great on a hot day like this."

- **Mix desserts and drinks.** Serving up an ice-cream drink, such as a root-beer float, is like a two-in-one delight that all patrons will love! You can serve it up in an old-fashioned glass, or give them a "to-go" cup to take it with them!

- **Offer the good stuff first.** Make it a habit for your servers to highlight the most expensive wine to your patrons. If it's a "by the glass" wine, selling for $20 each, then they may not feel as bad when they decline and order a $10 per-glass serving.

- **Create seasonal specials.** Drink items such as Cabin Fever Cure can go a long way to cure the winter "blahs." Made with Rumple Minze, vodka and hot cocoa, it's a sure-fired drink to become a hit with your customers.

- **Tea-based drinks are always a turn-on for summer.** Drinks such as iced Blueberry Tea – a combination of Amaretto, Grand Marnier and herbal tea – will delight your guests.

- **Create a sense of drama to sell more drinks.** Use dry ice, fun glassware, unique garnishes or unusual straws or containers to put some drama in the drinks that you serve. It's also a good way to advertise drink specials. When your servers walk through the dining area with colorful and unusual drinks on the tray, customers at the surrounding tables will surely notice and ask about those wonderful concoctions. Be sure your servers are well-trained and able to describe them tantalizingly to your customers.

- **Serve "to-go" insulated coffee mugs.** Many customers who come in for breakfast or brunch will want to take their coffee to go. Why not offer a slightly more expensive cup that they can take with them?

- **Sell drinks that don't stop.** If you sell a fun drink known as the Big Khauna Kola, why not offer free refills on it every time the customer brings it in? Chances are, most won't really bring in their cup, but they'll get to take it home and have a reminder of your establishment from then on!

- **Summer is a great time to create a festive atmosphere and sell more drinks.** If you have an outdoor patio or dining area, the warm, lazy days of summer present a wonderful opportunity to utilize it to the max. Make sure it's inviting – flowers, greenery, or even an outdoor fountain will entice your guest outside. They'll want to linger in the sun, or under the shade of a table umbrella or awning, to order more cool drinks and to relax.

- **Indoor "spectacular."** Even if you don't have an outdoor eating area, you can make an indoor dining area into an inviting haven. Fountains, flowers, greenery and ceiling fans can all contribute to make indoors seem like a tropical paradise. Keep in mind that summer is also a great time to offer exotic and refreshing new beverages rather than the same-old fare.

Let the Good Times Roll

Let your customers know that you really care. Appeal to the complete customer. Why did they come tonight? Is there a celebration? Let them know you're interested in their personal celebrations by offering a free drink, dessert or appetizer. Your guests will remember how they were treated and will surely return time after time. Here are some tips to increase beverage sales while also delighting your guests:

- **Don't just pump the ticket up; take your customers' needs and wishes to heart.** Put your energies into guest loyalty, not just getting more sales. Never use hard selling to try and convince customers to buy more beverages, especially alcohol. Remember that you might get an amazing tab tonight, but they may not return if they felt pressured or spent too much money.

- **Celebration?** When reservations are taken over the phone, that is a good time to ask if they will be celebrating a special event. Then, you can plan ahead to make their visit a celebration from beginning to end.

- **Don't assume the old adage that beer is a "man's" drink or that wine is for women.** Although beer is still ordered predominately by men, don't ignore women when it comes to offering a special on draft beer or a special brew from a microbrewery. Men enjoy a bottle or glass of wine with their dinners too. Many have become wine connoisseurs and are anxious to "show off" their knowledge. Give them the opportunity, and increase your sales and tips!

- **Feature exceptional drinks for holidays and special occasions.** Champagne has long been a drink that signifies "celebration" and it's also a high dollar item. Now that you can keep champagne fresh and bubbly overnight with the reusable bottle stoppers, consider a variety of champagne drinks to help your customers celebrate a holiday or event. You could also feature such champagne drinks as Mimosas (orange juice and champagne) with a morning brunch or French 75s (champagne with cognac or gin) as a celebration drink during Happy Hour.

- **Educate customers on worldwide cultures.** Start discussions about how the Europeans enjoy a nice port wine post-dinner and see how well it's accepted here in the States. Chances are, they'll see what all the fuss is about and want to adopt the same habits!

- **Have a built-in designated driver.** It may turn out that your patrons end up without someone to drive them home. If you realize that someone may not be fit to get behind the wheel, offer a free take-home and pick-up service so that nobody risks driving drunk.

- **Have a contest to get your customers' drink ideas.** Award a gift certificate for the most creative drink idea and then name the drink after the customer who thought of it. This simple gesture can be a great source of fun and goodwill among your guests and will also keep them coming back.

- **Your last name is a winner!** Every evening, you can draw a letter out of a jar and make that the winning letter for the night. Customers whose last names begin with that letter win a free appetizer for two!

- **Beverage tastings are always crowd pleasers.** Whether you decide to have a simple cheese and wine tasting or a microbrew tasting dinner, you'll raise beverage profits and create a perception among your customers that your restaurant is the "in" place and that you want them to have fun. Be sure to plan the event wisely. Will it be casual or formal? Will there be speakers on the types of beverages you're featuring? Check with your suppliers to see if they can help you with the proceedings and the cost. Most of all, make sure your servers are knowledgeable about the beverages you're serving.

How to Make Nonalcoholic Beverages Sell

Nonalcoholic beverages are becoming increasing popular. There are many reasons for this including healthier lifestyles, stricter drunk-driving laws and a general feeling that choosing nonalcoholic is "stylish." Provide what a growing number of customers want: a wide range of "smart" drinks. Here are a few tips for increasing your sales of nonalcoholic beverages:

- **Offer nonalcoholic specialty drinks to designated drivers.** Designated drivers don't need to feel left out of the festivities. Create special drinks that look and taste appealing. For a list of nonalcoholic beverage suppliers, visit www.allaboutpubs.com. Also, try www.nonalcoholicbeverages.com to find distributors of nonalcoholic wines and beers.

- **Use garnishes to make nonalcoholic drinks look tempting.** Kids love "Shirley Temples," made with 7-Up or Sprite and a splash of maraschino cherry juice to make it pink. Add a couple of cherries and you've got a winner. Serving nonalcoholic drinks in clever containers (like coconuts) will also get your customers' attention. Garnish them with fresh, tropical fruits and you'll soon reap the benefits in sales and profit.

- **Lessen your liability by training bartenders and servers how to suggest nonalcoholic beverages.**

Alcohol-related accidents can come back to haunt you if you don't teach your servers to watch out for potential problem drinkers. Knowing the correct dialog, such as, "You're the driver? I can whip up a great nonalcoholic version of (the drink). You'll never know the difference."

- **Use herbs and spices to liven nonalcoholic drinks.** For example, you could add a sprig of mint to an iced-tea drink or sprinkle cinnamon or nutmeg on a milk-based hot or cold drink to make them more colorful and appealing to your guests. Experiment with recipes to find out what your guests do or don't like. The site www.sasky.com features great recipes for nonalcoholic beverages. Keep on hand the ingredients for some of these drinks, a small inventory of nonalcoholic beers and wines and train your servers how and when to suggest them.

- **Suggest nonalcoholic drinks to your lunch crowd.** Your lunch customers are prime subjects to offer a variety of nonalcoholic beverages. Rather than simply "a glass of water," offer specialty waters such as Perrier. Teach your staff that even a glass of water cuts profits for you and tips for them. By the time the glass for the "water, please" is ordered, inventoried, washed and filled, you can run up to $1.08 in cost. And, it's "free" to the customer. That means no profit for you and no addition to the tab.

- **Be sure the bartender uses some of his or her flamboyant drink tricks with nonalcoholic beverages.** If your bartender is skilled in the art of mixing cocktails, be sure he or she uses the same skills for mocktails. Your bartenders should also understand the basic types of flavors and know how the different combinations interact.

- **Feature nonalcoholic wines on your wine list.** This will upgrade the status of a nonalcoholic wine. You can also feature other nonalcoholic beverages on your table tents and menus. For a great list of nonalcoholic wines that you can order, or to simply educate yourself as to the unique flavors of nonalcoholic wines, visit the Web site www.organicwines.com.

- **If you have a wine tasting party, set up an area for nonalcoholic wines.** The customers who don't drink alcoholic beverages will appreciate your thoughtfulness of taking them into consideration. They'll also realize that you offer these wines at your place of business and will probably order them next time they come for dinner. And don't forget to advertise the fact that you serve nonalcoholic wines and other beverages.

- **Visit Web sites such as www.probartender.com to learn about bartender software.** Some of these related sites offer recipes for nonalcoholic beverages that you might want to try in your restaurant. For example, a nonalcoholic Black Cow can be made with Sarsaparilla (root beer) and vanilla ice cream. Great kid pleaser – and you could feature it as "Black Calf" on your menu.

- **Stock your bar with items to help in nonalcoholic beverage sales.** Unique items such as fun-shaped and colored pitchers and cups and ice cubes that glow are all extras that you can use to promote either alcoholic or nonalcoholic beverages. Make any drink fun for your customers and they'll order more. See www.barsrus.com for a list of supplies, videos, bartending events and links to other bartender sites.

Extra Tips for Boosting Beverage Profits

There's serving a drink and serving a drink with flair and imagination. The following tips will help you impress your customers:

- **Charm your customers – and their drinks!** Here's something that's all the rage now – charms for your drinks! Each patron gets a special individually designed charm, made out of everything from silver to plastic, to adorn their glasses with so that nobody confuses drinks! You can either reuse the charms, or offer them as gifts for patrons to take home.

- **Colorize your coffee mugs.** Many patrons worry about whether or not they're really being served decaf or regular, and servers have a hard time keeping track of who's drinking what! To ease the worry on both sides, colorize your coffee service! For instance, blue mugs and a matching blue pot for decaf and red for regular!

- **Never run out of water.** One thing that is most complained about is that patrons were allowed to run out of their drink. Make sure everyone has an ice-cold glass of water on hand so that in case the server is extremely busy, they'll have a back-up beverage.

- **Long wait?** Drinks on the house! If someone goofed and your patrons' reservations are running a little late, be sure to offer free drinks to those in the party.

- **Hors d'oeuvres with every top-shelf drink.** You might design a special appetizer that goes well with your top-shelf drinks. Encourage customers to order top-shelf drinks instead of house labels.

- **Smack a logo on your mugs!** People will be more inclined to remember where they had that great concoction if you have your logo on the front of the cups.

- **Get crazy – get big!** Oversize your wine glasses and you'll find Happy Hour and dinnertime guests are falling all over themselves to partake of the goblet in which you serve wine.

- **Serve straws with everything!** Many patrons don't like the idea of drinking out of restaurant glasses on the lip of the cup. To appease those patrons, offer straws with everything – even small stirring straws with your coffee beverages.

- **Serve up a variety of "special-teas."** Tea is very popular now, especially green tea. Why not offer a variety of those teas in spiced versions, hot, cold, you name it?

- **Offer fresh-squeezed juices.** Instead of serving the regular boring juices, why not serve fresh-squeezed juices? They'll make a big splash with your breakfast and brunch patrons.

- **Serve your drinks in a "fishbowl"!** If a party of four comes in, they might want to order one of your beverages in a bowl! All you have to do is serve up oversized liquor mugs and stick as many straws as there are patrons in the group! It's a fun and intimate way to get to know each other.

- **Dab on a dollop of whipped cream.** Whipped cream is a smooth, creamy delight that goes well on hot or cold drinks! Serve it atop a steaming mug of hot chocolate or at the tip of an iceberg-like fruity drink!

- **Reinvent the rainbow!** With the liquors that are available today, you can serve up a drink in every color of the rainbow! It usually doesn't alter the taste of the drink much, but gives it a fun flair that your guests will appreciate.

- **Serve up shapely ice.** These days, ice cubes come in all shapes and sizes. If you have several special drinks you want to promote, serve them with fun-shaped ice cubes, such as hearts or stars. It gives the drink a nice effect and the women will love them!

- **Have special kids' cups.** We're not talking about a plastic cup with a lid on it, but an unusual one – one that they can paint or decorate themselves and take home with them. You can also serve the same kind of dishes, where they can color in the paper and snap it into the dishware itself. You can order these types of products from Neil Enterprises, Inc., 800-621-5584.

CHAPTER FIVE

COMPLEMENT YOUR ENTRÉES WITH SIDE DISHES

Making Low-Cost Side Dishes Look Appetizing

Even the most lowly of foods (consider the potato) can be spruced up to become an exciting complement to your entrées. One restaurant takes leftover mashed potatoes and forms them into delicate potato pancakes, then drizzles them with chive oil or an apple butter "beurre blanc" made with homemade apple butter. Here are some more great tips for giving low-cost side dishes that "added appeal":

- **Select and purchase the freshest ingredients possible for your side dishes.** It goes without saying that using fresh ingredients in your side dishes will not only enhance their presentation, but they will also taste better to your customers. For example, if you're featuring a vegetable soup on your menu, try to use fresh, not canned or frozen, whenever possible. Even garnishes must be fresh and appetizing. When it comes to side dishes, pay close attention to fresh!

- **Use seasonal items in your side dishes whenever possible.** If your town features a farmers' market, you have a great opportunity to purchase very fresh, "in season" fruits and vegetables and to create side dishes that reflect the seasons. For example, in the Fall, you might want to feature pumpkin soup, made with fresh pumpkin and real cream. Just as your entrées require that the meat is fresh, trimmed and/or seasoned properly, so do your side dishes. Pay special attention to the seasons and use them as a guideline for the side dishes on your menu. You can find many tips on seasonal recipes at www.shoeboxrecipes.com/html/seasonal.html.

- **Think of creative ways to present and serve side dishes.** Many soups can be served in hollowed bread bowls. You can also serve from hollowed vegetables. For example, guacamole can be served in a hollow avocado skin. This also cuts down on dishes that have to be washed. Consult your favorite cookbooks or visit Web sites such as www.gourmet.com for quick and helpful hints on preparing and presenting food.

- **Use simple accessories to dress up your side items.** Kitchen accessories can be used very effectively to add warmth and color to side items. A pretty woven basket with a clean, colorful cloth can be used to present rolls and bread and add a touch of elegance to your table.

- **Serve fresh foods such as vegetables and fruit on colorful skewers.** Containers and other items can be purchased at your local restaurant supply store. Or, you can visit Web sites such as www.katom.com to find what you're looking for.

- **Rediscover your "down home" roots when it comes to creating side dishes.** People everywhere seem to be moving back to familiar, homey cooking – the type of cooking that grandmothers and moms used to do in their own kitchens. Meatloaf, fried chicken, lasagna, are all comfort food entrées that can be paired with side dishes such as mashed potatoes and gravy, beans or garlic-cheese bread in order to set your menu apart from the rest. You can even add twists of your own to appeal to wider audiences. For example, the Riverview Restaurant in Kentucky tops its meatloaf with a tomato-onion relish rather than the typical gravy topping. Use your comfort-food memories as a guideline when thinking about creative side dishes.

- **Use the indigenous foods of your area whenever possible.** Every region has its own food preferences and the people are sometimes bullish about preparation techniques. For example, when the Northeast region of the United States comes to mind, we immediately think of things from the sea, such as Lobster Bisque and Clam Chowder. Side dishes, too, take their cues from the bounties of the region. The Northeast states have great abundances of corn, apples, cranberries and root vegetables, such as potatoes, beets and turnips. Take the region into consideration when adding new side dishes to your menu.

- **Advertise your side dishes in a way that will create a mental image.** Even if you don't have a photo of a side dish, you can create a mental image with words that will lure patrons to your establishment. Just be sure that your servings meet the expectations that you've created with the advertising. If you advertised fresh, steamed asparagus served with a creamy Hollandaise sauce, don't serve canned asparagus swimming in a dollop of melted margarine.

- **One way to make low-cost side dishes appetizing is to offer plenty.** Offer your guests "bottomless bowls" of side dishes that accompany your entrées. Mounds of mashed potatoes served in a large bowl or a steaming bowl of freshly-snapped green beans can make mouths water when served with a heaped platter of fried chicken.

Scrumptious Sidekicks!

Make sidekicks enhance as well as entice. You may have a great selection of superior entrees on your menu, but if your side dishes aren't up to par, the time, effort and money that you and your staff spent in creating the entrées can be wasted. Side dishes that complement your entrées are a vital part of your food service business. Restaurants around the world are beginning to give side dishes the starring role that they deserve on the menu – and with great success. Your guests expect well-cooked, delicious entrées no matter where they choose to dine, but if you can wow them with an unexpected, delectable side dish, the diners will often use that criterion to determine whether to return to your establishment. Based on a recent poll, 56 percent of restaurant customers say that they return to a restaurant because of the side dishes and 62 percent say they actually select an entrée from the menu based on the side dish that is served with it. There is no denying that side dishes are an important part of your overall menu planning. If your side dishes enhance your entrées, you'll make loyal fans of your customers. Try some the of following novel ideas for preparing scrumptious "sidekicks":

- **Potatoes rule!** Mashed potatoes, potato salad, au gratin, fried – potatoes have become a beloved side dish to our meals. There are so many different types of potatoes to choose from – white, golden, new, sweet potatoes, and more – all with their own distinctive flavors. Potatoes have even earned enough respect to have their own Web sites. You can pick up some great recipes and tips at Web sites such as www.idahopotato.com (they even offer a special Food Services site where you can access recipes, newsletters, fresh shippers' directory and even potato "clip art" that you can use in your menus or advertising). See www.potatohelp.com and www.oreida.com. You'll find a wealth of information from these and other sites available on the Web.

- **Take the "same old dish" and enhance it.** For example, glaze brussel sprouts with balsamic vinegar, sauté with garlic and shallots, then steam until tender. Top with toasted bread crumbs, and even kids will eat them.

- **Don't forget the salad.** In the USA, salads are actually considered an appetizer course. When customers finish their salads, the table is usually cleared and prepared for the main course. But in Europe, salads are served with the meal to aid in digestion. No matter when you serve salads in your restaurant, be sure that the ingredients are fresh and appetizing, and that you offer a variety of dressings.

- **A special "house" dressing can put your establishment on the map.** The Olive Garden restaurant is renowned for their "bottomless" salad bowl and garlic bread sticks; so much so that diners return time after time and just order that as an entire meal. Their special dressing is a hallmark of their salad, which is fairly plain. Use your imagination to create special dressings for your salads or visit Web sites such as www.kitchenlink.com or www.recipelink.com for recipes and ideas on how to improve your salad menu.

- **Offer seasonal vegetables as sidekicks.** As the bounties of the world become more easily available, in a shorter amount of time, we can sample fresh, seasonal vegetables from almost anywhere. If you have a local farmers' market, you can usually find fruits and vegetables that are in season in your area as well as those from another region. Make it a practice to offer seasonal vegetables that are prepared in unusual and attractive ways. They'll be popular accompaniments to your entrées.

- **Sidekicks are profitable!** You may think that entrées are the most profitable items on your menu. But side dishes have recently taken the lead in making a menu desirable to guests and profitable to restaurants. Profitable side dishes can be prepared from the most lowly of ingredients (potatoes, cornmeal and rice) and will enhance your main dishes and sometimes become the stars of your menu. Experiment with side dishes and be sure to keep track of their profitability.

- **Your customers will sense good value when you serve unusual side dishes.** When you offer an unusual side dish to complement an entrée, your customers will perceive it as good value. It's easy and inexpensive to dress up boring side dishes to become outstanding menu items that can even stand on their own. Visit the Copy Cat and Restaurant Side Dishes Recipe Index at www.about.com/food to get ideas about what will make memorable side dishes. The recipes and information are compiled from newsgroups and forums.

- **Grill or roast those veggies.** You can take almost any vegetable and make it a spectacular side dish by grilling or roasting it. Customers will love the taste that this method of preparation produces. They can opt to enjoy it as a healthful dish that stands on its own, or top it with a creamy sauce such as a spicy garlic tapenade.

- **Offer a wide variety of side dishes.** Variety, variety, variety! Just as each person is different, so are their tastes and preferences. Because the cost of preparing most side dishes is nominal, you can afford to offer a variety of items prepared in various ways. You'll soon discover which are popular and which are not and change your side dishes accordingly.

- **Breakfast side dishes are "hot" items.** Side dishes that are ordinarily served at breakfast (such as hash brown potatoes) are increasingly becoming popular items to pair with other meals of the day. Grits are served in the south in place of potatoes and omelets filled with side dishes such as fresh vegetables and topped with cheese or sauces are appearing on menus across the country. Experiment with serving typical breakfast side dishes with lunch and dinner entrées in your restaurant. Offer them prepared and served in unusual ways.

- **If your restaurant is ethnic, offer side dishes that complement.** If you're operating an Asian-style restaurant, grits or guacamole as side dishes probably aren't going to be too popular. Be sure that you target side dishes that will complement the other offerings in your restaurant. The site www.gourmetspot.com offers some great ethnic recipes for side dishes of all types, along with information from ethnic restaurants, recent articles about the restaurant and where you can buy tools and equipment for your kitchen. Another site, www.menu2menu, is a top information site for ethnic restaurants. It offers a comprehensive guide covering reviews, recipes, chef profiles, maps, suppliers, news, wines and market research.

- **Prepare side dishes to enhance the main entrées or to stand on their own.** The "old" way to think about side dishes is that they're only served to complement an entrée. But today's truth is that side dishes should be able to stand on their own, both in taste and presentation. Your customers should be able to order a favorite side dish à la carte. If you haven't already, begin to turn your thinking to making side dishes an integral part of your menu planning.

- **Cheese makes an excellent meal partner.** Cheese can become a star of any meal. Fried cheese, cheeses with dipping sauces, cheese straws, or simply a variety of cheeses on the side are all ways that you can enhance meals at your restaurant. In Europe, a cheese course is served after the main course and before dessert. American diners are increasingly becoming "cheese savvy" and are beginning to expect cheese on the menu. Familiarize yourself with cheeses and ways to serve them. Visit Web sites such as www.sargento-foods.com and www.ilovecheese.com to find out more about the various types of cheese, how to serve them and how to get them to work to the best advantage in your restaurant.

- **Servers should always be well-briefed on various side dish offerings** and their ingredients and preparation techniques. Knowledge of the side dishes you serve is the best way for servers to present and sell them. Chances are, your patrons will ask their servers about the ingredients in a dish or want to know how it's prepared. They may be asking because they have a health issue that prevents them from eating certain foods, or they may simply be curious. Hold meetings whenever a new dish is introduced to your menu and offer samples to your waitstaff so they can speak from experience when they recommend them.

Don't Forget the Garnish!

Paying attention to details when it comes to your side dish offerings is like accessorizing a wardrobe. You may be wearing the most expensive and stylish suit, but if you didn't choose an appropriate shirt and tie, the look is ruined. It's the same with side dishes – the garnishes are those important "accessories"! Keep it simple. Simple garnishes can both dress up a main dish or side dish and can also add flavor. The number-one concern when considering garnishes is to make sure they're edible. When selecting and preparing garnishes, also bear in mind the following:

- **Complement your dishes with garnishes.** When you think of garnishes for a side dish, think also of how it might complement the dish. For example, you might choose an herb such as mint leaves to garnish a rack of lamb. Visit the Web site www.garnishclub.com for more information about garnishes, such as using edible flowers, what to use with which dishes and even a gardening guide if you decide you want to grow your own herbs.

- **Be innovative and flexible.** For example, one chef serves strawberries marinated in balsamic vinegar, powdered sugar and vanilla extract as a garnish for his breakfast omelets. When strawberries aren't in season, he substitutes marinated grapefruit segments for garnish.

- **Use seasonal, fresh fruits for a colorful and healthful garnish.** When you place seasonal, fresh fruits on a plate, you're giving your customers added value. A wedge of watermelon can do wonders for a colorless platter of food. Add to that a few mint leaves and a strawberry or a spoonful of raspberries, and your customers will appreciate your efforts and expertise.

- **Garnish with spices for added color and taste.** Sprinkle paprika on simple mashed potatoes for instant color and zing. Offer fresh-milled cracked pepper for salads or pasta. You can even make your own croutons and offer them with soups or salads.

- **Freshly grated zest (for example, lemon or orange) makes a great garnish.** Zest from citrus fruits are natural garnishes for almost any type of food. They add color and pizzazz to dishes and drinks. They also add a healthful aspect to the plate. When you think about garnishes, be sure to consider zest.

- **Decorate your plates with garnishes.** The mark of true gourmet cooks is the ability to serve a dish that looks as appetizing as it tastes. But you don't have to operate a gourmet restaurant to make your dishes appear appetizing; you just have to know a few tricks of the trade. You can decorate with simple parsley or sculpted butter.

- **Other sources of inspiration.** Take a look at *The Art and Craft of the Cold Kitchen* by Chef Garde Manger (available at www.Amazon.com). This book is filled with ideas on how to make your meals more appetizing by using garnishes. *More Edible Art: 75 Fresh Ideas for Garnishing* by David Paul Larousse, (available at www.barnesandnoble.com) is also a great selection.

- **Your servers need to know about garnishes.** The more your waitstaff knows about garnishing food and drink, the more interesting dining experience your customers will have. During especially busy moments at the bar or dining area, the chef or bartender may be too busy or may simply forget to add garnish. If your waitstaff is trained to know what garnishes go with which food and drinks, they can easily add the touch of color or taste that is needed.

- **Edible garnishes can double as meal accompaniments.** Most servers think only of condiments as edible accompaniments to a meal, but garnishes can also be an accompaniment to many foods. Lemon or lemon zest can accompany fish, for example. Exotic fruits go especially nice with almost any meal and also add that "healthy" touch.

- **Drinks can benefit from garnishes too!** Everyone knows that a stick of celery goes great in a Bloody Mary. But why not try a stick of ginger? Lemon with tea is a known winner, but try something different by adding a stick of sugar cane (also good in lemonade). It doesn't cost much to dress up your cocktails with colorful umbrellas or bits of fruit on a festive pick. Experiment with garnishes and color and watch your customers gleam.

Appeal with Color

There are many ways that you can make side dishes into bright stars that will captivate and keep your customers returning time after time. Here are a few suggestions that may help you come up with some more ideas of your own:

- **Transform ordinary side dishes with a dash of color.** Use your imagination when it comes to presenting side dishes. Plain mashed potatoes can be presented with flair by serving them in their own ramekin, drizzled with cheese and a sprinkle of paprika to add some color.

- **Ambiance is everything!** No matter what type of food you serve at your establishment, remember that lighting influences the mood of the meal. Use flickering candlelight if you want your customers to linger over their drinks, appetizers and desserts. Correct lighting can even influence the form and texture of food. Be sure you consider which lighting should be used in your restaurant during your planning. You can order your candles in bulk at www.candlefactoryproducts.com.

- **Cookbooks.** Look at photos of side dishes in cookbooks and see how they're being presented. Remember that color makes a big statement in presenting lackluster side dishes.

- **Use colorful decorations to make your tables attractive.** A simple flower in a vase can greatly enhance the tables in your restaurant. Remember to use seasonal colors too – pine boughs during Christmas, orange flowers (or other type of decorations) for Halloween and Easter pastels to welcome spring. Your decorations can even be edible offerings of appetizers that your customers can enjoy the minute they're seated.

• **Clear dishes will let the colors of your servings shine through.** Using clear dishes for your servings is a great way to show off colors of food. A bowl of raspberries with whipped topping looks much more delicious in a simple, clear glass bowl, but its beauty may be lost if you serve it in a colored one. Use clear dishes to enhance all of your dishes, from appetizers to desserts. You can find clear dishware at www.recycledglassworks.com.

• **Use colorful vegetables as a side dish and to enhance a meat entrée.** You can sauté, grill, roast or steam vegetables, such as red and green bell peppers, carrots, broccoli and spinach, and serve them as a side dish to make your entrée plates come alive with color. You can even make a plain, green salad stand out by sprinkling some grated carrots or chopped green onion on top.

• **Sprinkle colorful spices on sidekicks.** Spices that enhance both taste and color are excellent choices to sprinkle on your side dishes to make them more attractive. For example, sprinkle a Cajun spice on baked potatoes to give them an extra zing and to make them stand out on the plate.

• **Condiments add color to any dish.** Colorful condiments can be used creatively to add color and kick to almost any dish. For example, you can create a mustard or ketchup "smiley face" on a child's plate. Salad dressings, such as Raspberry Vinaigrette, can be swirled around a salad plate, or sprinkle colored sugar around a dessert plate.

- **Make your desserts stand out with added color.** Add a dollop of whipped cream and then some colored sprinkles to make your desserts sparkle. This extra bit of color and flavor can mean the difference between the desserts in your restaurant being "ho-hum" and "talked about."

- **Don't be afraid to add color and taste to vegetables.** Your vegetables, no matter how plain, can really stand out if you use your imagination to add a bit of color. For example, you could add a dollop of sour cream and then sprinkle it with curry, parsley or paprika. Use colorful vinaigrettes to add some zing and make those blah veggies attractive.

- **Colorful herbs can also enhance your side dishes.** From parsley next to an entrée or a sprig of mint on top of a whipped dessert, herbs are always a good choice to add color and taste. You can even grow your own herbs very inexpensively. Your customers will appreciate the taste and color that the herbs will add to their meals. Order your own herb garden at www.goodearthliveherbs.com/order.htm.

CHAPTER SIX

ADDING DECADENT DESSERTS TO YOUR MENU

Delicious Desserts = Big Profits!

Save room for dessert? Apparently, many diners are doing just that! If your restaurant hasn't already jumped on to the dessert bandwagon, it's time to do so. Recent statistics plainly show that dessert sales in restaurants are on a rapid rise and show no signs of slowing down. Popular restaurant chains are developing desserts to sell pre-packaged to other restaurants, grocery stores, mail order, or directly to the customer from the restaurant. Refine your dessert menu now and reap the considerable profits that desserts can bring to your business. Here's how:

- **Consider going all out by hiring a pastry chef.** Pastry chefs are in hot demand, so you'll probably pay dearly to employ a good one! Or, you could buy pre-made, frozen dessert items from top brands like Marie Callender or The Cheesecake Factory.

- **Appetites for desserts soar as sales increase.** Dessert sales are booming and sophisticated diners are demanding them. With today's convenience products, such as "thaw and bake," you don't necessarily have to pay a pastry chef to be successful in the dessert phase of your restaurant. You can also buy ready-made desserts from the ever-increasing number of companies that cater strictly to restaurants. Order some delectable treats at www.dessertstodiefor.com.

- **Follow the trends.** Statistics point to the dessert boom continuing indefinitely. Technomics' Jackie Dulen says that there are two main reasons why: More sophisticated consumers is one reason. These diners are willing to take "culinary chances." This fact has spurred a new crop of pastry chefs who are continually setting new trends in their work. Whether or not you can afford a pastry chef, go with the trend and be sure that your business offers the best desserts you can manage.

- **Be sure to offer low-calorie desserts such as fruit.** Low-calorie fruit and "sugarless" items are in great demand in restaurants. As people watch their diets more carefully or deal with health problems that prevent them from eating sugar or high-calorie foods, restaurants are coming up with creative ways to make these types of desserts appetizing. Using fresh fruit instead of canned is always a good idea – and sugarless sauces are easy to make and add another dimension to an otherwise bland choice.

- **Today's conveniences allow restaurants to serve high-quality desserts at a high profit.** Cheesecakes from The Cheesecake Factory or pies from Marie Callender's can be sent to your restaurant in a minimal amount of time, thus increasing the quality and convenience of being able to offer signature desserts. There are also "thaw and bake" items that can be prepared in a miniscule amount of time. You can even add your own special touches so that even the most simple of desserts becomes a much-talked-about item among your diners.

- **The "Grand Finale" is as important as "Fantastic Beginnings."** The "complete experience" for your diners definitely includes a top-rated dessert. You can strive to provide the best appetizers and entrées, but if your desserts fail to impress, the customers will leave disappointed. Pay attention to the quality of your desserts.

- **A great dessert will make a lasting impression on your customers.** More than likely, your customers will remember, above all, the last thing that they eat at your restaurant. That's why the importance of dessert cannot be minimized on your menus. You can't expect to buy a frozen turnover, heat it and stick it on a plate with some whipped cream and have customers want to return for the "experience." Think of desserts as a way to make lasting impressions on your diners and to increase your profits.

- **Give a classic dessert a special twist.** Even plain apple pie can be updated in new, trendy ways. Add nuts or raisins to the filling and a piece of melted cheese on top rather than ice cream. Think of new ways that you can give your tried-and-true desserts a "lift" and watch your dessert sales increase.

- **Simple is better when it comes to desserts.** Simply made and served desserts can always perk up your sales. If your restaurant is designed to appeal to families, try gelatin desserts or pudding. A beautifully molded dish of flan, swirled with caramel and served on a clear glass plate is a dish that will appeal to your customers' sense of taste and vision alike.

- **Smaller is better too!** For the more petite appetites, have your servers offer "half" helpings of your desserts. Even if you offer a discount for the smaller servings, your profit margin will increase on overall sales.

- **Experiment with textures – from lusciously creamy to crunchy.** Try adding various types of nuts to a creamy dessert. Experiment with your desserts so that you can offer a change from the norm. Ask your customers which they prefer.

- **Cheese can add a creative touch to many desserts.** Cheese has always been a mainstay for any meal, but when you add it in a creative way to desserts it becomes a taste sensation. Try adding various textures and tastes of cheeses to your desserts and have your waitstaff try them and compare them to the "old" method of preparation.

- **Dessert drinks, both alcoholic and nonalcoholic are great profit items.** Don't forget dessert drinks when planning your dessert menu. They are extremely high-profit items and can be much more appealing to those diners who may not want a more filling dessert. Dessert drinks can also be very appealing visually. An Amaretto Coffee served in a glass cup with a dollop of whipped cream and a cherry on top can be very appealing. Non-alcoholic drinks can also be visually appealing. Serve your hot cocoa with whipped cream and a sprinkle of cinnamon or nutmeg on top. A great dessert for a cold winter day.

- **Make desserts fun** – both in looks and presenta-tion. If you want your restaurant to appeal to kids, you'll want the best part of the meal (to a kid) to look festive and fun. Kids are more apt to love the "special effects" of the dessert as much as the taste. But grown-ups are more sophisticated in their tastes and in what appeals to them visually. They are much more into taste and textures. Ice cream sundaes with a wide variety of sprinkles are a delight for children, while an adult may enjoy Crème Brulee with a citrusy crust.

- **Make your desserts look so good that your customers will "ooh and ah-h-h" when they're presented.** If you manage an upscale restaurant, you may want your desserts to appear as "works of art." Family restaurants may prefer to court their customers with sizeable portions and big dollops of whipped cream or gooey caramel or fudge that cascades down the dessert. Whatever your dessert style, remember that this part of the meal – the finale – needs to be thought out and brought together using items that will appeal to your customers.

Promoting Desserts

Monetarily, profits on desserts can make up for losses on other menu items. A great dessert can make up for a mediocre meal, both in satisfaction and profit. The ingredients are usually inexpensive; labor is where you incur the greatest cost. Nevertheless, desserts normally have a 20-percent food cost and they can help cover more pricey items on the menu, such as steaks and fish. Take every opportunity, therefore, to promote your dessert selection; your efforts will pay dividends! Consider the following possibilities:

- **Implement a "dessert program" to increase sales.** A dessert program can be as simple as Boston Market's idea to offer a free dessert if the waitperson doesn't ask "Would you like dessert?" Another could be to offer a free appetizer or drink if you order a dessert at the beginning of the meal. Boston Market has seen a 10-percent increase in their dessert sales since they implemented the program.

- **Gentle suggestions can be big "nudges."** Your waitstaff doesn't have to be a group of hard-core salespeople to push the dessert items on your menu. Gentle suggestions at the beginning of a meal such as, "Before you order, I want to let you know that we're featuring a great new dessert today – New York-style cheesecake with a fresh blueberry topping." That will open the door to an after-the-meal "nudge" such as, "Have you decided to top off your meal with our cheesecake special?"

- **Try offering desserts for two and watch your sales increase.** If your customers seem reluctant to order a dessert, try offering two spoons or forks with one dessert. It doesn't seem quite so indulgent when you're sharing. What if one customer wants one type of dessert and the other wants a different one? Place "half-helpings" of different desserts on the same plate. Your diners will be delighted.

- **Tips can double on a single ticket** if you sell more desserts. Desserts are high-profit items, and on the final ticket, they can increase your tips too. Have your waitstaff keep tabs on their tickets for a period of time, say, a month. Then, have a meeting, tabulate the tips on tickets with dessert items and those without. Seeing is believing, and your waitstaff will strive to sell more desserts when they realize that it's money in their pockets too!

- **Serve-yourself dessert bars are very popular.** Whether your restaurant is family-style and you offer a sundae bar with all the toppings or you offer a fine-dining experience, you can increase your profits by setting up "help-yourself" dessert bars. These are becoming as popular as salad bars throughout the country, and your customers will appreciate being offered a variety of desserts from which to choose.

- **Suggest dessert "extras."** Dessert "extras," such as a scoop of vanilla bean ice cream on top of hot apple pie or a dollop of whipped cream on top of that strawberry shortcake, can be appealing suggestions to your guests. Be sure to have plenty of extras on hand and teach your waitstaff how to suggest them.

- **"Your" personal favorite is a great selling tool.** People love a recommendation that comes from actually trying the product. Be sure that your waitstaff has an opportunity to try all of the dessert items on the menu and then encourage them to recommend their favorites to your customers.

- **Ways to make your on-site desserts profitable.** If you decide to go all out and hire a pastry chef to make your own signature desserts, you can make them highly profitable by selling them to outside vendors and other restaurants. Selling whole desserts, such as cheesecakes, pies and cakes, can greatly increase your profits while advertising your own restaurant's brand. Marie Callendar's now works with a line of 32 pies and has been able to keep the quality of the pies by freshly baking them at each restaurant location rather than using a separate bakery or commissary.

- **Suggest "best-selling" dessert items.** Be sure that your servers know the best-selling dessert items on the menu. Passing that information to your customers is also a great selling tool when they're trying to decide which dessert to order.

- **Suggest and serve desserts with lots of humor.** The meal is winding down and your diners are trying to decide which dessert to order. Fun remarks such as, "We've taken all the calories out of that hot fudge sundae" or "You only live once - don't live without dessert," can gather smiles from around the table and make your customers more inclined to order a dessert. Serve the desserts with humor, too, and your customers will leave with a good feeling.

- **Be knowledgeable about the desserts offered.** As in other side items on your menu, servers need to be completely knowledgeable about desserts. From texture to ingredients, knowing how to explain a dessert to your customers is an essential function of your waitstaff. Many customers will want to know about a dessert item for health reasons, possibly allergies. Some will just want to know out of curiosity. Have your waitstaff observe how desserts are made and always offer samples.

- **Take a "no excuses" attitude when it comes to desserts.** You can have a "no excuse not to order a dessert" attitude without being pushy and alienating your customers – especially if you do it with humor. You can always suggest "sharing" and then bring extra plates and forks or spoons. Carry-out containers are also a great way to get customers to order desserts.

- **Place dessert trays strategically.** Dessert trays are great to display desserts to more than just the table you're serving. A dessert tray that is strategically carried through the restaurant so that other diners can view the offerings is a great way to get them thinking about ordering dessert before they've finished their other courses.

- **Offer whole desserts such as pies and cakes to go.** Many restaurants nationwide are offering whole desserts to take home or back to the office. Large parties may order a whole dessert to continue the party back home. This is a great profit-maker and also a great way to advertise your restaurant after the customers leave.

- **Make your customers feel as if they deserve dessert.** Dessert is known as a "treat" and most people treat themselves to indulgences if they feel they "deserve" it. "It's your birthday," "It's Friday," "Congratulations on your promotion," or simply, "You've had a busy week," can be suggestive catalysts for your diners to order dessert. Teach your waitstaff to pay attention to tables and how to find out if there is a celebration or even complaining about what a rough week it's been. It makes suggesting desserts much easier.

- **Display table tents that feature professional photos of your dessert items.** A colorful table tent is an especially good way to display photos of dessert items. They are on the table when your customers first arrive and get them thinking about desserts before they place an order. Desserts are colorful and appetizing and they photograph well. They are a great choice if you plan to use table tents in your restaurant.

- **After-dinner dessert accompaniments.** Some patrons may not want a real dessert, so be prepared to offer them a dessert coffee, and if you want to, include a small trinket of chocolate on the side of the saucer!

- **Dessert samplers make the sale!** One of your choices might be a dessert sampler – where guests get to try out a bite-sized taste of all of your various indulgences.

- **One dessert "made for two" will delight your guests.** Restaurants are taking advantage of the trend to "share" desserts and are actually advertising desserts "made-for-two." These special desserts can be a bit larger than a dessert offering for one and served on one plate with two forks or spoons. Even when sold at a discount, you'll realize a profit from the sheer number you'll sell.

How to Showcase Your Desserts

A "ho-hum" attitude about desserts can ruin your dessert sale profits. But, when approached with enthusiasm, desserts can be a huge profit-maker for your business. The following tips will help you make the most of your desserts:

- **Draw a mental picture.** Use lots of adjectives. Using adjectives that whet the appetite is essential when suggesting dessert items. Luscious, creamy,

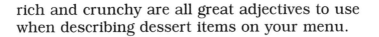

rich and crunchy are all great adjectives to use when describing dessert items on your menu.

- **Have meetings where your servers sample desserts.** Ask them to write down the adjectives that they would choose to describe the taste and texture. Encourage your staff to be enthusiastic when presenting them to your customers. Offer a prize for the most creative "wordsmith." Then, encourage your servers to go out and use those adjectives when describing desserts to your customers.

- **Keep your customers informed about special desserts.** Chalkboards at the entrance to your restaurant, table tents and well-trained servers are all excellent ways to inform your customers about dessert offerings. If you advertise in the community, be sure to mention dessert specials or new desserts in your ads.

- **Offer plain vanilla ice cream with lots of toppings from which to choose.** You don't have to have a world-renowned pastry chef to have appealing desserts. Plain vanilla ice cream appeals to almost everyone, and be sure to keep lots of toppings and sprinkles on hand to dress it up. You can even use alcoholic beverages such as brandy and whip up a thick and delightful "Brandy Ice" served in a brandy snifter or champagne glass to make a more sophisticated dessert item.

- **When you take your customers' entrée orders, suggest that they leave room for dessert.** One restaurant sells their hot blueberry and cherry cobbler specials by letting their customers know that they must order it when they place their entrée order, because it's baked fresh and extra time must be allowed. Or, if you suggest a wonderful dessert before your diners order, they can be thinking of the dessert throughout the meal.

- **Whet appetites by describing the aroma of certain desserts.** Aromas wafting from the kitchen have sold many desserts. Your waitstaff can also use aromas as a selling point for desserts by describing the aromas to your customers. Smells of vanilla bean and apple pie and cinnamon evoke memories of childhood and dining satisfaction.

- **Dabble in the sweet stuff!** Powdered sugar makes a great impression on guests when you dust the plate with it, and then lay the actual dessert on top of it. You can also lay a cutout on the plate, then dust it with powdered sugar, and when you remove the cutout, you'll have a wonderful design!

- **Serve chocolate-covered platters.** If you buy the old-fashioned ketchup and mustard squirt bottles, you'll have your own chef's style decorating tool to create wonderful design in chocolate right on the plate. It's best to lightly draw on the outer edge of the plate, and make sure servers know to keep their thumbs out of the sauce!

- **Dazzle them with raspberry drizzle!** Raspberry sauce goes well with just about any dessert – even chocolate! You can use the same technique to design a beautiful reddish drawing on the dessert platters before you drizzle a bit of the sauce right on top of the actual dessert.

Special-Occasion Desserts

Desserts are great items to promote and get your restaurant noticed. If you have dessert items that set you apart from the rest, think about catering them for special occasions. There are many ways that you can promote desserts. A special display case at the entrance – with your desserts artfully arranged – takes full advantage of promoting desserts as soon as your customers enter your restaurant. If you have freezer room, you can offer frozen desserts that clients can take home and thaw and eat when wanted. Here are some other ideas for promoting your special dessert items:

- **Encourage your customers to order family-size "special occasion" desserts to take home.** Special-occasion desserts that can be picked up and taken home are growing in popularity as our nation becomes busier with work and home. People want quality and quantity for their hard-earned bucks. Offerings such as a "bucket of ice cream" with the order of a birthday cake is a great idea – and it might keep mom or dad from having to stop by yet another place to pick up ice cream to go along with the cake. Whether the occasion is a birthday, family reunion or candlelit dinner for two, sending desserts home can be a great profit-maker for your restaurant.

- **Have a "Sundae Sunday" special.** Sunday dining at a restaurant is becoming as firm a tradition as a big Sunday dinner at home used to be in days gone by. A simple idea that will delight your guests and is easy to set up is a sundae bar. To make it really special, offer it only on Sundays and watch the families flock in. If you don't want to set up a bar where your customers help themselves, advertise your Sundae Sundays on chalkboards, an outdoor marquee or table tents. Be sure to have plenty of toppings and sprinkles on hand!

- **Promote seasonal "special" desserts.** Holidays are perfect opportunities to offer seasonal-type desserts. This is a time to let your imagination soar – you could offer pumpkin cake with sage ice cream for Halloween or peppermint ice cream and a scrumptious Lane cake for Christmas. Go to the Web site www.restauranthospitality.com to find numerous recipes and articles about seasonal desserts.

- **Be sure that you have specialty items on hand to go with your desserts.** Always have items such as candles, syrups, sprinkles, berries and nuts on hand for your desserts. Specialty dishes such as for sundaes and banana splits are great to show off your dessert items. If you cater to kids, keep specialty items such as twisted straws and "character" spoons on hand to make them feel special.

- **Christmas is a great time for special dessert offerings.** Christmas is a perfect season for you to try new and different dessert items. Your customers will be in a more festive mood and more willing to "make room for dessert." Try something different from the norm, such as eggnog pudding or plum pudding, rather than the usual pumpkin pie or chocolate cake. You can file away some fabulous holiday finds at www.christmasrecipe.com.

- **Start a free birthday or anniversary club and offer a free dessert.** If you can get people to sign up for a birthday club, you get to capture their address, which means you'll be able to mail out coupons and other offers to increase traffic to your establishment. About a week before their birthday, send them a coupon for a free birthday cake and then serve them a miniature-sized cake when they come in to celebrate!

• **Make your usual desserts festive at holidays by using garnishes.** Garnishes such as cherries, colorful fruits or herbs are perfect additions to your holiday desserts. Try twisting flexible, black licorice sticks into "scary" shapes for Halloween, or tint your whipped cream topping with food coloring. Use garnishes throughout the year to make your desserts memorable.

• **Offer "take home" desserts for holiday gatherings.** Holidays are especially hectic for families who work and try to shop and cook for holidays. This is a great time for you to really promote whole desserts for holiday gatherings and increase your dessert profits. Pies and cakes are easy to transport and will keep better than desserts such as ice cream or custard desserts. People want that "down home" taste, so if you make your own pie crust, for example, be sure to advertise the fact.

Desserts with a Difference

Competition is stiff in the dessert "arena." You must always try to keep one step ahead with new and innovative ideas. Use the following suggestions to trigger you imagination:

• **Kids like it gross.** Instead of offering the same-old brownie with ice cream, serve up worms in dirt!

You heard it right: serve chocolate pudding with crushed Oreo cookies on top. Then, make sure a few gummy worms are "crawling" out of the top of the concoction.

- **Appeal to dieter's remorse.** Women and men alike don't simply want to share a regular dessert – they want to eat healthier! Why not offer one or two diet desserts that are made with skim milk or other low-fat ingredients? That way, they can indulge without worrying about a bulge!

- **Cater to those who are fond-of fond-ue!** Fondue desserts are popular with grown-ups and kids alike. Bring out the table-top fixings and watch everyone enjoy their after-dinner decadence!

CHAPTER SEVEN

USING SIDE ITEMS TO ATTRACT FAMILIES

Party Fun for Kids

When it comes to attracting families to your restaurant, consider kids as a main factor in the equation. At first glance, catering to families with kids may seem more trouble than it's worth. But, if you succeed, it will be worth your while in the profits you'll realize and the customers you'll gain – not just now, but for years to come. In a recent poll, over 55 percent of adults stated that their children have significant influence over which table-service restaurant they choose. Over 47 percent of adults said that the kids actually choose the restaurant. Clearly, if you want families in your place of business, kids should be considered in every aspect of your planning. Atmosphere, menus, entertainment and pricing all combine to influence kids and their parents to dine in your restaurant establishment. Bear in mind the following issues when trying to attract kids:

- **Appetizers make ideal kids' "meals."** Kids usually don't have enormous appetites, their attention span is minimal and if something looks good, they'll probably try it. That's where using side items to attract families comes into play. A small plate of appetizers, garnished with unusual veggie cutouts in the shape of animals, will get the kids' attention – as will special beverages and fun desserts. The payoff for your planning will be a busy dining area with wall-to-wall families with kids. Don't under-estimate the influence of kids in your business.

- **Use side items to plan and promote special occasions for kids.** You don't have to wait for the holidays to have a special-occasion party for kids. They celebrate every day as a party day – and if you want more families in your restaurant, you will too. For example, have a silly drink day, featuring special, fruit-based drinks, garnished with fun items such as exotic fruits or sticks of peppermint or sugar cane. Serve the drinks in unique containers or add reusable silly straws.

- **Offer special kids' treats for special holidays.** Have a Santa or an Easter Bunny come in for an hour to pass out candy canes or jelly beans for dessert. This will allow the parents to linger a bit longer over dinner and order an adult dessert or an after-dinner drink. On days such as Mothers' Day, when you know business will be at its peak, set up TVs and VCRs and prepare special side items that the kids can munch on while mom and dad enjoy their meal in peace. You can order your staffers some costumes at www.costumeworld.com.

- **Halloween is a great time to offer specialty kids' items.** Kids love Halloween, but parents are more than a little reluctant to have them wandering the neighborhood, trick-or-treating at strangers' homes. You can take advantage of this by offering a safe-haven Halloween party for parents and kids. Offer special, "scary" snacks, create "chilling" drinks by using dry ice. Decorate and add some inexpensive door prizes and you'll end up with a great party – and return customers.

- **Offer free desserts, drinks or appetizers on kids' birthdays.** If you have a special corner (or room) of your restaurant that could be devoted to use as a "party" area, consider having birthday theme parties for kids. Parents can make the reservations and you can offer (for a special price) cake, drinks and perhaps a variety of snacks from your menu. It's a good way to promote new business and get your side items noticed.

- **Teach your servers how to promote side items to kids.** If a server has a bad attitude towards kids, the parents and the kids will probably feel uncomfortable during the meal and – worst of all – won't come back! But, if you teach your servers to treat kids as human beings and not merely something to be dealt with, you'll surely attract more families to your place of business. For example, be sure that your servers point out the unique side items on the kids' menu and perhaps offer a special treat, such as a balloon, at the end of a meal.

- **Celebrate special kids' days by offering special side items.** For example, celebrate "back to school day" by advertising a free apple (for the teacher) with an order of apple pie à-la-mode. It's also a great day to advertise your restaurant by offering colorful pencils printed with your business's name.

- **Don't forget nutrition when it comes to creating your side items.** Make nutrition fun by offering healthful snacks, desserts and drinks served in fun containers or carved into funny shapes and sizes. The parents will appreciate your efforts to help teach their children about healthful eating.

- **Concentrate on making kids' side items into finger foods.** Kids love finger foods and dips. Be sure you provide a wide variety of side items, from chicken strips to French fries and fresh veggies.

- **Advertise kids' side item promotions.** Lure
  parents and kids to your restaurant by offering
  freebies on specialty items. Promotions, such as
  "all-you-can-eat side dishes when you order an
  entrée," can be a great calling card for kids who
  would much prefer a second helping of macaroni
  and cheese or a free dessert rather than roast beef
  or fried chicken.

- **Holiday side items for kids.** Holidays are great
  opportunities to promote side items for kids. In
  fact, holidays are also indulgent times for adults
  and kids alike. You can have a Christmas cookie
  contest and let the kids decorate their own
  cookies. Parents and kids alike will enjoy an
  Easter egg hunt and a price-fixed brunch
  afterward. Use your imagination and suggestions
  from your servers to think of ways to promote
  holiday side items to increase profits.

- **Focus on other special days besides "holidays."**
  You don't have to concentrate on major holidays to
  promote side items for kids. Special days like
  Grandparents' Day can be great to offer a "Kids
  with grandparents get a free dessert" deal. Look at
  your calendar or search the Internet for special
  days to promote your side items. The site www.offi-
  cialholidays.com will give you a thorough listing of
  all the major and not-so-major holidays.

Fighting Boredom and Disruptions with Side Items

If the kids are being "entertained" then the parents are likely to linger longer – and bump up the tab. So, it's in your best interests (and the interests of all concerned) to fight the boredom factor by laying on a few "distractions." Consider the following:

- **Offer snacks and activities designed especially for kids.** Besides the usual fare of coloring mats and crayons, your restaurant can set itself apart by offering small toys or books. But if you're planning to offer toys with special promotions or kids' meals, don't offer junk. Kids are smart and know the difference. You can order yours at www.kidztreasures.com.

- **Special kids' snacks.** Simple snacks, like veggie chips (crispy, healthful, baked snacks) with a small serving of a popular dip or ketchup and a special drink served in fun containers with a "crazy" straw, are good items for keeping the kids entertained.

- **Think of ways to make your kid customers feel more grown up.** For example, offer mocktails for kids, featuring extra cherries, drink umbrellas and swizzle sticks. And don't forget the catchy names. Brainstorm with your waitstaff to come up with ways to appease kids while appealing to their parents.

- **Offer coloring mats picturing your special side items and a variety of crayons.** This is a tried-and-true method of keeping kids entertained before and after the meal. Most kids like to color, and if they're coloring a particularly delicious or fun-looking side item, they'll be more likely to want it when you take the order.

- **Contests are great ways to keep boredom at a minimum – and to promote your side items.** Coloring contests (with no limits on entries) featuring drawings of your specialty items can be used to encourage repeat business. The winners can be notified by mail and win a specialty side item of their choice.

- **Games are great kid-pleasers too!** Cracker Barrel features simple puzzles at every table. Your vendors should be able to help you with this; both monetarily and with their products' promotions. You can find table games and more at www.extextoys.com.

- **Use television or movies and snacks to keep kids occupied.** Setting up a corner of your restaurant as a play area or an entertainment center can attract kids as well as parents who want to enjoy a good meal "sans" interruptions. Offer popcorn while they're watching, or better still, offer appetizer items that appeal to kids. Get them to try new and different things. You can order your very own popcorn machine at www.snappypopcorn.com.

- **Entertain the kids by letting them see the preparation of food items.** If you have an open kitchen, offer mini pizzas and let the kids watch you make them to their specifications. Or, bring items such as desserts tableside and offer an array of favorite sprinkles for their ice cream or whipped cream. Beverages, too, can be prepared tableside with added drama provided by your waitstaff.

- **Balloon popping discounts are a hit with kids.** They choose from a group of balloons, and "win" whatever item is on the coupon inside! Free desserts. Free fries. You name it! Order your balloons in bulk at www.bubblesofjoy.com.

Appealing to Families

A friendly, informal atmosphere, where entire families – large or small – are made to feel truly welcome, is the key to attracting family groups. Here are some suggestions:

- **Entertainment is a great way to attract families.** You don't need a ten-piece orchestra; a clown who creates funny shapes out of balloons will delight the kids in your restaurant. Set up a corner and have a cookie cutting party, offering a specialty drink or dessert as a prize for everyone who participates. Meanwhile, mom and dad can relax and order more wine or appetizers while the kids are having fun.

- **Price your side items so that families can eat there without breaking the budget.** Chili's Bar and Grill is a success mainly because it caters to families and it doesn't cost a lot of money or take a lot of time to dine there. Service is fast, and they offer booth seating, which is often desirable for folks with kids.

- **Have family days that feature low-cost side items.** If your restaurant isn't attracting families as much as you'd like, try promoting a family day, featuring appetizers and special beverages at a lower cost. You could set up a hot dog stand with lots of different toppings for the kids or a sundae bar where the kids could make their own desserts after dinner. A family day could also be a "kids eat free" day.

- **Remind your customers about family occasions they want to remember.** Offer a discount to customers who use your personalized reminder service. It doesn't have to be a birthday or anniversary. It can be any special event that brings families together.

- **If you have an extra room, keep it open for special family groups.** Promote the facility to customers organizing family reunions. Come up with a handy promotion, such as if the group has over ten participants, give them one free drink.

CHAPTER EIGHT

SIDE ITEM PROMOTIONS TO GET YOUR RESTAURANT NOTICED

Stay Ahead of the Competition

Actively market your appetizers, desserts, side items and beverages. It doesn't matter how wonderful your fare is if people don't know about it. There are many other "wonderful" restaurants competing for your business, so you have to be leaps ahead in promotions and advertisements in order to get your establishment noticed. Side items are great to promote, because they can be unique and add so much diversity. Even if you serve a fare of steaks, chicken and seafood, the side items that accompany them can become the driving force in getting customers to return time and time again. Side-item promotions can be as simple as a glass display case of special desserts at the entrance of your restaurant, or as complicated as bottling your own sauces and toppings and marketing them outside your restaurant. Here are some useful tips to help you stay ahead of the competition:

- **Market your unique identity.** Decide which side items make your restaurant unique and then think of ways to promote them, depending on the amount of time and money you have to spend. Remember, you have to think ahead to stay ahead of the competition. If you need help on how to market signature items, visit the Web site www.restaurant.org for advice and suggestions.

- **Sell packaged signature items inside your restaurant.** If you have some room in your restaurant, consider setting aside a space for signature items. The space could be as simple as shelves behind the checkout counter or as elaborate as a separate retail "store" area. Signature items that you can sell include bottled sauces, private-labeled bottled wine and baked or frozen items

- **Think of promoting side items outside your restaurant.** If you have a signature item that you're especially proud of and has put your business "on the map," you may want to consider offering it in a retail market such as a grocery store or special-foods catalog. Restaurants' signature items are also appearing in malls as well as being sold in kiosks and major department stores.

- **Be a trendsetter.** "Smoothies," for example, are hot! If you've thought about selling smoothies in your restaurant, now is the time to cash in. A growing trend in the smoothie market is to make them with medicinal herbs. *Entrepreneur Magazine* lists "Cold Stone Creamery" as one of the fastest-growing franchises. Smoothies are their biggest selling item. For more information, plus some great recipes, visit the Web site www.recipezaar.com.

- **Use promotional items that advertise.** When you plan for promotional items, be sure that they will advertise your restaurant after your customers take them home. T-shirts, mugs, gift certificates and anything else you can think of that will have your business name emblazoned on them are great advertisements. The Web site www.promomart.com

contains useful information and products for you to consider.

- **Think of ways to get free press coverage.** Major cities will have a food section in their local newspaper. Contact the food editor and ask if he or she would like to cover a special appetizer extravaganza that you're having, where you'll be testing a wide range of new starter possibilities.

- **Gift certificates are a great way to advertise and increase sales.** Restaurants that offer gift certificates bring in clients who might not have heard about your restaurant or found the time to try it out. The Internet provides a way to order gift certificates at the site www.giftcertificates.com. You may also have access to local sites that offer gift certificates. Consider placing your restaurant on the "gift certificate" list.

- **Catering can put your business ahead of the rest.** When corporations, families, clubs and other types of organizations host get-togethers, they depend on catering in a big way. Catering takes your business to another level and is yet another good way to get your place and your menu items noticed. NACE (National Association of Catering Executives) has a helpful Web site at www.nace.net if you're considering catering for your restaurant. NACE offers such information as a "bookstore" that features books on how to plan and operate a catering business, articles on catering and the location of the nearest NACE chapter.

- **Distribute coupons for side items.** Local businesses, churches and nonprofit organizations appreciate discount coupons to distribute to their members. You can also place coupons in a local newspaper. Be sure that your waitstaff is informed of and honors the coupons when presented.

- **Work with cab and bus drivers to get business during conventions.** When people come in town from all over the country (or the world), they'll need advice on where to eat. Offer an incentive to cab drivers who refer their clients to you, such as a free dessert, or entire meal, if necessary!

- **Get help from your vendors** to promote your various appetizers, desserts, side items and beverages. Your suppliers can be a great source of help when you have a promotion. One restaurant had their suppliers help them in an advertising campaign where prices were "rolled back" to the '60s. It was a month-long event that offered daily prizes and the culmination prize was a free trip. Your suppliers should be eager to help you in any advertising campaign that features their products and can even help you with ideas.

- **Loss leaders are a great way to create traffic.** Why not offer a meal for a $1 when you buy one at the regular price? This is an especially effective method for times that are statistically not busy.

- **Advertise a luncheon fashion show.** Enlist a local boutique to have a fashion show at lunch. Be sure to let everyone on your customer database know about it. And don't forget your suppliers and local merchants. Serve an impressive array of exciting side items.

- **Add patrons to the wall of fame.** Start a contest where customers are given a card that is punched every time they come in and order a beverage or appetizer. At the end of every month, take the top person who ordered the most of that item and place their name on the wall of fame award. Of course, they'll have to have an incentive to do it, so be sure to throw in a free meal for their continued patronage.

- **Know when local hotels or convention centers are hosting groups.** Keep in touch with the community happenings and you'll find all sorts of ways to advertise your restaurant. Offer discounts or coupons to attendees. If you have a marquee, welcome the groups by name. You can get a list of many conventions at www.geocities.com/ TimesSquare/4677.

Menu Makeovers

Revise, update and re-assess your menu – regularly. What was popular, even a couple of months ago may be out of favor today. Also, an item that looks good on a menu won't necessarily be a good selling item. Always be on the lookout for fresh, innovative ideas to improve your menu. The following ideas offer "food for thought" for updating your side repertoire:

- **Seek professional or peer help when planning your menu.** There are many sources from which you can choose in order to avoid common mishaps when planning your menu makeover. See the Web site www.nrn.com for information on where to find professionals to help you enhance your menu.

- **Tapas menus are a hot trend** in today's dining establishments. Consider introducing a separate tapas menu; the perfect showcase for a wonderful array of savory appetizers. Tapas menus are no passing phase; they're here to stay so use the concept to increase your appetizer sales. The custom began many years ago in Spain when the bartender would cover their customers' drink glasses with meat or vegetables as a way to keep flies from landing in the drinks. Since that time, tapas menus have evolved as a way to get customers to experiment with new tastes and textures. Tapas also appeal to the small appetites and weight-conscious. To get the full story on today's tapas menu trend, visit www.nrn.com/operations/toro/htm.

- **Create new signature items that will shine on your menu.** Highlight items on your menu that made you go into the restaurant business in the first place – and those that have helped you develop a loyal customer base. When you introduce a new item on your menu, highlight it also, but carefully monitor the results it brings.

Take Your Guests on a Gourmet "Trip"

Invite your customers to join you on a culinary adventure. Feature items on the menu that reflect another region or country. For example, you might have a weekend or night where you feature a special menu that includes items from Italy. "Mile-high lasagna," a salad made with Calamato olives together with Tiramisu for dessert will tantalize and delight your guests. Here are some other great ideas for broadening your guests' epicurean horizons:

- **Use decorations to create the mood.** Transform

your restaurant with decorations to make your customers feel they are really on a dining adventure. Use color, texture and items that are indigenous to the area. For example, for Mexico the colors should be bright and vivid. Perhaps, hang piñatas from the ceiling and drape serapés over the chairs. Order them at www.allpinatas.com.

- **A taste of your city.** Team up at a mall with several local restaurants that offer slightly different fare and showcase all of your talents with a Taste of (Your City Name). Locals will love it and out-of-towners will appreciate sampling the regional dishes.

- **Go "regional" with your desserts.** Regional desserts can be fun and varied. Tiramisu might be offered with an Italian fare or flan with Mexican food. Always popular are the "homemade" Southern desserts such as peach cobbler and pecan pie. If you vary the entrées at your restaurant, match the desserts to the "region" of the entrées. Your customers will feel like they're on a dining "trip" from appetizer to dessert.

- **Serve menu items in special dishes or glassware.** Check with your suppliers to see if they will let you have (or help you acquire) special serving dishes for your theme "trip." Margarita glasses for a Mexico theme can be purchased very inexpensively, and guacamole can be served attractively in half of an avocado shell. Beer could be served in Bavarian "Bier Kruge" (large beer mugs).

- **Theme restaurants are becoming very popular.** It doesn't have to be a particular era. Theme restaurants can be based on geography as well! In

Grapevine, Texas, one restaurant resembles a tropical rain forest – right down to the live parrots they use to entertain the crowd. Serve local delicacies, accompanied by a glass of the regional wine.

Follow Up on What Pleases Your Guests

Monitoring your menu results is as important to your business as training your waitstaff. It's important to keep track of items and how they're selling – or not selling. Here's how to gather the data and apply the results:

- **Build a customer database.** Capture your customers' names and addresses and enter them into a database for future promotions. You can also ask for opinions about menu selections and offer a discounted purchase for those who respond. One way to get your clients' names and addresses is to have a guest book for them to sign. When they sign, give them a free drink or dessert card for their next visit.

- **Use your customers as a "sales force."** Customers love having their opinion valued. Not on a plain-old postcard, but when an owner or manager comes up to ask them personally about it. Use their feedback as a way of testing out which methods will be tried and true – and which will be deadly duds.

- **Use draw cards and/or business cards to increase your customer database.** Have people fill out cards with their names and addresses or collect business cards in a giant brandy snifter.

About once a month, send a mailing and offer an incentive such as a free dessert or appetizer when they return to your restaurant. This method will not only increase traffic, but it will also keep the name of your business circulating.

Some Low- and No-Cost Employee Motivational Programs

What most motivates the people who work in your restaurant is recognition, not money! This section is full of some great ideas from other businesses. You do not need to spend a lot of money (or any at all) to let employees know how much you appreciate their efforts. Reward your employees and they will reward you and your business back many times over the small cost and effort exerted.

- **Treat your top performing employees the best!** Create and foster an atmosphere of "employees who do the best, receive the most rewards!"

- **Eliminate "but" from your vocabulary.** Whether you are counseling an employee, giving them a pat on the back, or a combination (You are doing great, but...). Your employee just forget everything positive before the BUT, and will only remember the negative that comes after it.

- **Focus on the top.** Don't spend 85 percent of your time paying extra time and attention to the bottom performers, and all but ignore your top performers. They may tend to feel the lack of attention is due to their performance and may negatively change work habits. Concentrate on your mid–upper-level performers. Encourage their growth and development – the bottom of the food chain will likely go elsewhere.

- **Positive reinforcement of top performers will return even greater performance.**

- **Cut loose your sea anchor!** A sea anchor is a nautical term for a sail which is dragged behind a vessel in the water to slow or stop forward movement. While this principle worked great in the 1,800 sailing years – that principle of carrying dead weight will slow or drag down even the best organization, and ultimately cost you profits and employees. Cut the anchor loose!

- **Avoid cash awards.** Sounds crazy but think of it this way: Cash awards go directly into a paycheck. Most employees don't share this information with coworkers. Instead, present gift certificates in your company (returning the business to your company), and present with a plaque or other award. A plaque on a wall is a constant reminder to the employee and others that you recognize top performance – now that gift certificate or time-off award you presented your employee is truly valuable – and the knowledge of what top performance can gain an employee is common knowledge.

- **Challenge employees!** Even the best employees need to be challenged. Don't settle for the same performance, same tasks, day in and day out. Challenging employees does two things: it builds confidence and better employee satisfaction as they accomplish more difficult tasks and grows future leaders for your organization by challenging them beyond normal levels.

- **If you insist on cash rewards – specify the terms.** A great example is an incentive program which rewards employees with cash assistance to purchase a computer. This small reward will pay dividends for years by allowing employees additional training on computer use (on their own time), as well as serve as a constant reminder every time they use the computer of what the company did for them! This builds loyalty and ultimately performance.

- **Develop non-cash-related rewards programs,** some may include:
    - Suggestion programs (to reduce costs)
    - Employee of the month
    - Timeliness rewards
    - Rewards for working extra shifts
    - Successfully completing training regimen
    - Free movie tickets
    - Thank-you letters/thank-you e-mails
    - Designated parking spot
    - Free merchandise (T-shirt with your logo – this is free advertising!)

- **Develop more cash related rewards programs,** some may include:
    - Free dinners
    - Free gas, oil and lube change certificate
    - Time off
    - Gift certificate (home improvement, electronics, books)

- **Personalize gifts.** Take the time to write a hand-written congratulatory note. This goes a long way in comparison to the computer-generated thank-you note your secretary types! Personalize plaques with their name and even their photo, etc.

- **Incentive program ideas may include:**
  - Safety program (identify/remove safety hazards – how much does an accident cost you?)
  - Mystery shopper programs
  - Loyalty incentives (1 year of employment, etc.)
  - Cleanliness program
  - Rewards for guest comments and surveys (perks programs – three positive comments = four hours off!)

- **Informal awards/recognition programs.** On-the-spot awards. The idea is that you don't have to take it to vote, to the board, to the awards committee, etc. Empower management to give out on-the-spot awards (cash, time off, etc.). Employees know managers have this power and will rise to the occasion to earn the rewards for their hard work.

- **Pat-on-the-back awards.** These are the kind that cost nothing, and usually return the best results. Pat-on-the-back awards are just that; quick, informal and certainly appreciated by employees. A perfect example is telling the kitchen staff that the meal they prepared was delicious. That is true job satisfaction!

- **Pins and button rewards.** Pins, buttons and other trinkets for the employee to proudly wear (Employee of the Month, Best Overall, Best Smile, etc.). Low-cost, but high return in satisfaction, plus your employee shares the award with everyone with which he or she comes into contact.

- **Group activities.** Morale Day cookouts, barbeques, beer bash, etc. Make it during the normal work day for a double bonus – time off and a great party! This has several benefits: it shows you care, it allows management to socialize with employees and gives you an opportunity to bond (prove you are human too!).

- **Showcase employees.** Have you seen those Wal-Mart commercials featuring Wal-Mart employees? Yes, those employees are real; they appear as a reward for superior performance.

- **What are the best ways to reward your employees for superior performance?** Money, recognition by management, time-off awards, advancement/promotions, prizes and gifts.

- **Work in the trenches.** As a manager, show you care about your employees and what they do; show them that you are willing to perform their job as well. This shows an interest and dedication to your employees, and builds and invaluable trust.

- **Ensure employees know their role in your organization.** Ask the dishwasher what he does. If he replies, "Washes dishes," you have some work to do. If he replies, "Ensuring the restaurant can properly function by providing a constant supply of clean dishes," you have succeeded. Every person in the organization is important and has a critical role. Each person serves as a cylinder in the engine – if one cylinder fails, the engine falters, and so does your business.

- **Recognize your people in public.** Recognition behind closed doors loses the power of the presentation; an audience remembers recognition!

Here's a comprehensive list of today's tastiest appetizers, specialty drinks and desserts.

APPENDIX

W̲e scoured the food service community and came up with a current list of hot and trendy appetizers, specialty drinks and desserts that both the chains and independents are using right now. Don't be left out!

Appetizers

A SEAFOOD SALAD - Octopus, squid, shrimp and fish; tossed with fragrant herbs on a bed of beanthread noodles.

ASIAN CUCUMBER & GRILLED EGGPLANT SALAD - Sweet and sour peanut sauce, chili jam, crisp sesame cracker.

BABA GHANOUJ - Grilled eggplant mashed with sesame sauce (tahini), yogurt, lemon juice and garlic; topped with olive oil.

BABY GREENS SALAD - Mixed mesclun greens with goat cheese and roasted sweet peppers; tossed in a honey, Dijon and balsamic vinaigrette.

BAKED BRIE - Fine imported French cheese; baked in puff pastry and served with seasonal fruit.

BARBECUED SHRIMP - Jumbo shrimp filled with smoked sausage; wrapped in country bacon and broiled with a zesty BBQ sauce.

BASIL CHEESE TORTA - Cheese torta prepared with fresh basil pesto, cream cheese, sun-dried tomatoes and roasted pine nuts; served with sliced French bread.

BAYOU PEARLS - Crab and angel hair pasta crispy fried over sauce of buerre blanc.

BEEF BALL ON STICKS - Beef ball on sticks roasted on skewer; topped with sweet and sour sauce.

BRUSCHETTA - Fresh-baked bread topped with fresh tomato, garlic, olive oil and basil.

BUFALA MOZZARELLA CAPRESE - Imported with tomatoes and basil.

BUFFALO QUESADILLA - Served with orange sour cream, salsa and guacamole.

BUNDNERFLEISCH - Thinly sliced cured beef; served with cornichon and pearl onions.

BUTTER-POACHED NEWPORT LOBSTER - Lobster gently poached in rich butter; served over cardinal whipped potatoes and baby spinach.

CAJUN MUSHROOMS - Whole mushroom caps stuffed with a Cajun sausage stuffing, deep fried in beer batter; served with a mustard sauce.

CALAMARI - Fresh calamari lightly battered and fried to a golden brown; served drizzled with a caper buerre blanc sauce.

CARPACCIO DI MANZO - Slivers of raw beef with arugula and shaved parmigiano.

CHARBROILED OCTOPUS - Topped with virgin olive oil, fresh garlic and fresh lemon.

CHAR-GRILLED PORTOBELLO MUSHROOM - With jumbo lump crabmeat and garlic parsley beurre blanc.

CHICKEN AND MUSHROOM STUFFED PASTRY - Puff pastry stuffed with white meat chicken and mushrooms.

COCONUT BREADED PRAWNS - With a sweet, spicy mango dipping sauce.

COCONUT SALMON - Salmon chunks dipped in beer batter then rolled in coconut, deep fried; served with a sweet and sour plum sauce.

COCONUT-FRIED SHRIMP - Beer-battered jumbo gulf shrimp with fresh coconut; served with pineapple/ shiitake sauce.

COQUILLES CREOLE - Sea scallops lightly seasoned in cajun spices and blackened; served over a tomato and basil vinaigrette.

CORN-FLOURED FRIED CALAMARI - Crisp and golden brown, with tomato basil, salsa and chipotle mayonnaise.

CRABCAKES REMOULADE - Sautéed fresh lump crabmeat, Louisiana remoulade sauce.

CRAB-CRAYFISH CAKE ON MIXED GREENS WITH GREEN-APPLE ROSEMARY VINAIGRETTE - Fried cake made from crabmeat, crayfish, scallop puree, eggs and bread crumbs; served on mixed greens dressed in a green apple-rosemary vinaigrette.

CRABMEAT AND ROCK SHRIMP RAVIOLI - In tomato-lemon grass broth.

CRAB-STUFFED SHRIMP - Jumbo shrimp and crabmeat stuffing, baked and presented with a lemon beurre blanc.

CRISP DUCK SPRING ROLLS - Braised shredded duck and shiitake mushrooms in a crisp wrapper; orange, ginger and toasted sesame seed dipping sauce.

CRISPY PAN-SEARED FLYING FISH - Fresh fruit and vegetable-curried cole slaw drizzled with lemon-infused oil.

CURRIED LAMB EMPANADAS - Empanadas filled with a curried lamb, toasted pecans and raisin filling in a parmesan crust; served with a cilantro-coconut-yogurt dipping sauce.

DEEP-FRIED SHRIMP BALL - Deep-fried shrimp ball with hot, spicy chili on the side.

DOLMADAKIA - Marinated grape leaves stuffed with rice and beef or eight vegetarian grape leaves made with rice, dill and olive oil; both are served with Tzatziki sauce.

DRUNKEN NACHOS - Black beans, Jack and cheddar cheese, jalapenos, guacamole, sour cream, tomatoes and tequila lime chicken.

DUNGENESS CRABCAKES - Served over fresh sautéed greens with a red bell pepper aioli.

EGGPLANT LOCICERO - A Napoleon of breaded eggplant served with crawfish and shrimp in a vodka-dill cream sauce.

ESCARGOT AUX CHAMPIGNON - Sautéed escargot with shallots and garlic tucked in mushroom caps.

ESCARGOT BOURGUIGNONNE - Garlic, tomato and artichoke with red wine demi glace in puff pastry.

ESCARGOT STUFFED MUSHROOMS - Mushroom caps stuffed with escargot, baked in a garlic butter and white wine sauce; served with jalapeno cheese bread.

ESCARGOTS - The finest French gastropods, broiled in a mushroom duxelle with butter and garlic.

FALAFEL - Vegetarian combination of ground chick peas, parsley, garlic and spices deep fried; served with tahini.

FETTUCCINI WITH WILD MUSHROOMS - Porcini, shiitake and oyster mushrooms tossed with fettuccini.

FILE GUMBO CUP - True Cajun-style gumbo made with a dark rich roux, Cajun vegetables, andoulle sausage and shrimp; served with a jalapeno corn muffin.

FRIED BRIE WITH SEASONAL CHUTNEY - A wedge of breaded and fried brie; served with seasonal chutney and sliced French bread.

FRIED CACTUS - With tomatillo salsa and garlic dipping sauces.

FRIED KIBBEE - Minced sirloin and cracked wheat blended with unique spices; stuffed with ground sirloin, diced onions and pine nuts.

FRISSEE SALAD - Tossed with toasted pistachios, sliced pears and crumbled Great Hill blue cheese, dressed with a homemade sage vinaigrette.

GRAPE LEAF ROLLS - Stuffed with rice and ground sirloin.

GRAVLAX - House-cured salmon, fresh dill and lemon, crispy scallion potato cake, poached beets and crème fraiche.

GREEN CHILE PORK STEW - Topped with Monterey Jack cheese and buttered tortillas.

GRILLED ASPARAGUS AND ROASTED TOMATO SALAD - With chive oil and crisp, fried shallots.

GRILLED CRUSTINI WITH ROASTED GARLIC AND BRIE - Grilled crustini served with a clove of roasted garlic and baked Brie; served with demi glace.

GRILLED KING TRUMPET MUSHROOMS - Marinated grilled king trumpet mushrooms, grilled scallion, truffle oil and mushroom demi glace.

GRILLED, MARINATED PORTOBELLO MUSHROOM - Served with bruschetta, roasted garlic and rosemary-infused extra-virgin olive oil.

HALIBUT BEER BATTER - Halibut chunks dipped in beer batter and pecans, deep fried; served with home fries and a cocktail, béarnaise sauce duo.

HALIBUT CEVICHE - Halibut marinated in lemon and lime juice mixed with fresh vegetables and cilantro; served in an avocado half.

HALIBUT CHUNKS - Tender chunks of fresh Alaskan halibut dipped in Alaskan Amber and cashew beer batter; deep fried and served with French fries and tartar sauce.

HERB MARINATED GRILLED SEA SCALLOPS - Crispy vegetable julienne and a seasoned fruit sauce.

HONEY-SEARED PORK TENDERLOIN - Slices of sweet pork tenderloin accompanied by a caramelized onion and tomato tartlet.

HUMMUS - Mashed chick peas blended with sesame paste and lemon juice; topped with olive oil.

JALAPEÑO POPPERS - Breaded jalapeño halves stuffed with cream cheese and served with Ranch dressing.

JAMAICAN MEAT PIES - Flaky fried pies with savory filling of ground beef, tomatoes, onions and Caribbean herbs and spices; served with cilantro-lime.

KOO CHAI - Soft rice biscuit stuffed with Chinese vegetables, served with sweetened black soy sauce; choice of deep fried or steamed.

KOTOPITA - Boneless rotisserie chicken blended with fresh mushrooms, peppers and Greek herbs, wrapped in flaky filo pastry and baked.

LETTUCE WRAPS - Thai specialty with chicken, ginger and water chestnuts over rice sticks; served with lettuce cups, Chile garlic and soy mustard sauce.

LOBSTER AND BUTTERNUT SQUASH BISQUE - Lobster meat, young greens and toasted pumpkin seeds.

LOBSTER, SHRIMP AND LUMP CRAB COCKTAIL - Lime, mint and tomato vinaigrette.

MANCHAC CRAB CAKES - Lightly seared Louisiana crabmeat cakes in beurre blanc sauce.

MIENG KUM - Tangy citrus-marinated sashimi-grade salmon with sweet peppers, chiles, red onions and cilantro; served with Cuban bread croutons and baby greens.

MINI MARYLAND CRAB CAKES - Presented with a honey Creole mustard sauce garnished with fried capers.

MINIATURE QUICHE - An assortment of bite-sized quiche (Classic French, Florantine, Mushroom and Ham and Swiss).

MOZZARELLA SAPORITA - Boconccini wrapped in prosciutto with braised radicchio.

MUSHROOM AND CHICKEN LIVER PATE - A creamy, smooth, subtle combination of fresh chicken livers, mushrooms, butter, brandy and seasonings.

MUSHROOM AND SPINACH CREPES - In roasted garlic cream salsa of pickled onion and tomatillos.

NEW MEXICO FONDUE POT - With barbecued lamb and pistachio bread.

ORGANIC MIXED GREEN AND STRAWBERRY SALAD - Shaved fennel and mixed greens, fresh strawberries tossed in creamy strawberry dill dressing with mint-walnut oil; served with rhubarb, apple and green peppercorn chutney.

OYSTERS BAYOU - Freshly shucked oysters, lightly floured in mild Cajun seasonings and pan sautéed; served over a bed of spinach and drizzled with a spicy bayou sausage cream sauce.

OYSTERS BIENVILLE - Four fresh oysters baked with crabmeat, cheeses and herbs.

OYSTERS GIOVANNI - Lightly fried Louisiana oysters; served with a painted, stained glass of five sauces.

OYSTERS MESCALERO - Fresh oysters fried in masa and presented with a chili pepper sauce, crispy tortilla strips and spicy corn relish.

PATE DE FOIE DE CANARD - Smooth mousse of duck liver; served with warm toast and fresh fruit.

PIPERIES FLORINIS - Roasted peppers stuffed with cheese and fresh herbs.

PLANTAIN TORTE - Sheets of whole wheat tortilla layered with sweet plantain and creamy cilantro-tofu; served over a spicy watermelon-tomato salsa with red pepper romesco.

POLPO ALLA GRIGLIA - Baby octopus drizzled with lemon and olive oil.

PORTABELLO MUSHROOM RAVIOLIS - Served with pesto and marinara sauce.

PORTOBELLO CON CAPRINO - Grilled with goat cheese, arugula and chopped tomato.

POTTED SMOKED SALMON SPREAD - Alaskan smoked salmon blended with cream cheese, butter and fresh dill; served in a small crock with sliced French bread.

PROSCIUTTO, FONTINA, RICOTTA AND ASIAGO SACHETTINI - Pasta purses filled with Fontina, Ricotta and Asiago cheeses and Proscuitto.

QUESOS CON AMOR - Reggianito, sharp cheddar, port salut, havarti and gargonzola cheeses; served with grapes, olives and bread.

RACLETTE BAKED RACLETTE CHEESE - Served with pearl onions, cornichon and potatoes.

RADICCIO, ENDIVE AND WATERCRESS SALAD - On Boston lettuce leaves with sherry-Dijon vinaigrette and a tomato, basil and garlic toast.

ROULADE OF SMOKED SALMON - With olive goat's cheese, pickled zucchini and soy sesame oil.

SAGANAKI - Melted Kassari cheese made with sheep milk, battered and sautéed in olive oil, then flambéed with brandy and sprinkled with fresh lemon.

SATAE - Marinated pork or chicken in a mixture of Thai spices on sticks; served with white toast, peanut sauce and cucumber salad.

SAUTÉED CALAMARI - Tossed with cherry tomatoes, crushed chili pepper and garlic.

SCALLOP-STUFFED MUSHROOMS - Mushroom caps stuffed with scallops, baked in a garlic butter and white wine sauce with white onions; served with jalapeno cheese bread.

SCALLOP-STUFFED MUSHROOMS ROCKEFELLER - Same as the scallop-stuffed mushrooms with an addition of rockefeller sauce, spinach and pernod paste; with béarnaise and parmesan cheese.

SHRIMP AND CRAB BISQUE - Fresh from the sea with a touch of cream and cognac.

SHRIMP MARGARITA - With mango, papaya, cilantro, lime juice and a splash of tequila.

SHRIMP PIRI-PIRI - Very spicy, from Mozambique, sautéed with garlic, lemon and cayenne pepper.

SHRIMP SAGANAKI - Sautéed large shrimp, feta cheese, tomatoes and scallions in a hot herb sauce.

SHRIMP-STUFFED AVOCADO - Chopped shrimp and vegetables mixed with Thousand Island and remoulade sauce; served in an avocado half.

SIZZLING GARLIC SHRIMP - Jumbo shrimp in garlic-rosemary butter sauce with Cuban bread for dipping.

SKILLET GRATIN OF CRAWFISH TAILS - With pearl onions and soy beans.

SMOKED ALPERS TROUT - Served with warm, fresh crepes, fresh fruit and greens a strawberry horseradish sauce and a balsamic herb vinaigrette.

SMOKED CHICKEN AND PICKLED SHRIMP SPRINGROLLS - Springrolls filled with smoked chicken, pickled shrimp, jicama, basil and chives; served with a cucumber relish, a black pepper caramel and toasted sunflower seeds.

SMOKED DUCK QUESADILLA - With sweet peppers and smoked gouda cheese.

SPANAKOPITA - Spinach and feta cheese wrapped in flaky puff pastry dough and baked.

SPICED TOMATO CHUTNEY - Two rounds of breaded fried mild goat cheese; served with a chutney made from sweet ancho chiles, spiced fresh tomatoes and toasted pecans.

SPICY FRIED ZUCCHINI - Zucchini strips with a spicy coating, deep fried; served with a sour cream-horseradish sauce.

SPINACH & ARTICHOKE DIP - Spinach, artichokes and roasted peppers in creamy cheese sauce with garlic crostini.

STUFFED ARTICHOKE HEARTS - Wrapped in prosciutto, stuffed with fresh herbs and goat cheese.

SWEET PEPPER CALAMARI - Lightly breaded, tossed with red wine vinaigrette, sweet cherry peppers, banana peppers and pepperoncini; with garlic aioli.

TASSO SHRIMP - Four charbroiled Gulf shrimp wrapped in tasso with mango butter.

THINLY SLICED, MARINATED TUNA - Served with a

pickled cucumber salad and whole grain mustard vinaigrette.

TUNA CARPACCIO - Poppy seed-encrusted tuna with capers and roasted peppers.

VEGETABLE PLATTER - Fresh tomato wedges, carrot sticks, cucumber slices, celery sticks, mushrooms, mild Greek peppers, broccoli flowerettes and a large bowl of Ranch dressing.

VEGETABLE PUFF PASTRY - A mixture of garden vegetables wrapped in puff pastry.

VEGETARIAN GRAPE LEAF ROLLS - Stuffed with rice, tomatoes, green onions, parsley, lemon juice and olive oil.

VIETNAMESE-STYLE LOBSTER AND SNOWCRAB SPRINGROLLS - Served with sweet and hot dips.

VONGOLE AL FORNO - Baked clams with seasoned bread crumbs.

ZUPPA DI COZZE E VONGOLE - Mussels and clams steamed in a garlicky wine sauce.

Specialty Drinks

AMARETTO ALEXANDER - Amaretto, creme de cacao and vanilla ice cream.

BAHAMA MAMA - Rum, creme de cassis and pineapple, lemon and orange juices.

BERMUDA RUM SWIZZLE - Bermuda's favorite combines Goslings Rum, tropical juices and a touch of Falernum.

BLUE WAVE - Bombay Sapphire, Blue Curacao and a splash of lemon juice.

BRANDY ALEXANDER - Brandy, creme de cacao and ice cream.

BREEZE - A cool passion fruit flavor with amber rum

CHERRY SLURPEE- Blended cherry brandy, sour mix and grenadine.

CHILE 'RITA - An exotic blend of "Besito Caliente" blackberry Habanero sauce, lime juice, Hornitos 100-percent agave tequila and Coutreau served on the rocks.

CHOCOLATE BANANA CREM - Banana liqueur, creme de cacao and ice cream.

CHOCOLATE RASPBERRY TRUFFLE - Stoli vodka, Godiva chocolate liqueur, Chambord and a chocolate garnish.

CITRON PINK LEMONADE - Absolut citron, sour mix, and a splash of cranberry carribean champagne.

COCOA MOCHA CREME - Kahlua, creme de cacao and ice cream blended and topped with whipped crème.

CRAN 'RITA - This frozen beauty is a blend of our La Posta 'Rita and Ocean Spray Cranberries.

DARK AND STORMY - Goslings rum and ginger beer.

DESERT ROSE MARGARITA - José Cuervo Gold tequila, fresh lime/lemon juice and prickly pear cactus.

ELECTRIC MARGARITA - Midori, tequila, triple sec, sweet and sour with wedge of lime.

ESPRESSO MARTINI - Stoli vodka with Kahlua, Frangelico and a shot of espresso.

FLAMING COFFEE - Kahlua, triple sec and brandy flamed with coffee and fresh whipped cream.

FUZZY LEPRECHAUN - Peach schnapps, blue curacao, vodka, orange and pineapple juice.

GRUMBY - Midori, vodka, sour mix and 7UP.

HORNY 'RITA - Hand shaken margarita, made with Sauza Hornitos 100-percent agave tequila, Cointreau, sweet/sour, and freshly squeezed lime juice.

INDIAN SUNRISE - Tequila, mango and grenadine blended with sweet and sour.

INDIAN SUNSET - Rum and amaretto mixed with pineapple, cranberry and lime juice.

JAMAICAN-ME-CRAZY - Pusser's Rum and coconut rum, with a mix of tropical, cranberry and lime juices with a dash of grenadine.

JEN ZEE VODKA - Tonic, fresh grapefruit juice Kir Momentum-Stoli Raszberi, Chambord and a splash of Prosecco.

LIGHTNING - An electrifying blend of vodka, orange juice, and pineapple juice topped with burgundy wine.

LUSCIOUS LOU LOU RONRICO - Gold rum, Myers dark rum, orange juice with a squeeze of lime, served blended.

MAI TAI - Light rum, dark rum, triple sec, orange juice pineapple juice, creme de noyaux.

MANDARIN MARTINI - Absolut mandarin vodka, grand mariners, orange juice.

MANGO TANGO - Mango, rum, cream of coconut, grenadine.

MARTELL VSP STINGER - Made with Martell Cognac and Marie Brizard Crème de Menthe in a brandy snifter.

MARTINI - A double made with Bombay gin, served up and perfectly chilled.

MESILLA MIMOSA - Gruet Brut champagne mixed with cranberry and orange juice.

MICHELADA - Dos Equis Lager over ice and spiked with a shot of lime juice.

MIMOSA PROVENCAL - Grand Laurent champagne laced with orange juice and a touch of triple sec.

MINT JULEP - Bourbon and simple syrup over crushed ice with mint.

OLYMPIC SIDECAR - Metaxa Brandy with triple sec and fresh limes. Served with a sugared rim.

ORANGE CRUSH - A delicious blend of fresh orange juice, Smirnoff Vodka and triple sec. Topped with an orange slice.

PINK LEMONADE - Fresh-squeezed lemonade with vodka and a touch of grenadine.

PURPLE FLIRT - Dark rum, blue curacao, sour mix pineapple juice and grenadine.

QUEEN CITY KAMIKAZE - Fresh limes with triple sec and vodka; served in a glass shaker to strain and pour.

RAINBOW - A colorful drink of grenadine, vodka, blue curacao and sweet and sour mix.

RED ROSE - Ketel One vodka, Cockburn's port and a splash of lemon and cranberry juices.

RUM RUNNER - Rum, blackberry brandy, DeKuyper's® Banana Liqueur.

SEA BREEZE - Vodka, cranberry and grapefruit juices.

SEX IN THE JUNGLE - Rum, peach Schnapps and tropical juices.

SINGAPORE SLING - Gin, cherry brandy, lemon juice, soda water, grenadine.

SKYLAB - A mixture of rum, vodka, apricot brandy and blue curacao.

SMOKING MARTINI - Ketel One vodka, dry vermouth and a splash of Glenlivet.

SQUALL - Light rum and green passion juice.

SUNRISE - Grey Goose L'Orange, Grand Mariner and a splash of orange juice.

TEQUILADA - Made with gold tequila, real pineapple juice, half and half cream and coconut cream.

TEQUINI - José Cuervo Especial, Grand Mariner and a splash of lime juice.

THE "SHRIMPTINI" - Absolut Peppar, dash of tabasco sauce and grilled shrimp.

THE HELPING HAND - Stoli vodka, Chambord, Grand Mariner and a splash of citrus.

THE ITALIANO - Vox vodka and a splash of lemonade.

THE MADRAS- Stoli Ohranj, Finlandia Cranberry and a splash of orange juice.

THE PINKO - Stoli Persk, Raszberi and Ohranj and assorted fruit juices.

THE SCORPION - Ronrico silver rum, Paul Masson brandy, orgeat syrup and sweet and sour with orange juice, served blended.

THE SHARK'S TOOTH - 151 Bacardi rum, sweet and sour and grenadine.

THE ULTIMATE - Grey Goose vodka, peach grappa and a splash of Prosecco.

TYPHOON - A mixture of vodka, peach schnapps, raspberry schnapps, cranberry and pineapple juice.

VOODOO JUICE - Cruzan banana rum, coconut rum, pineapple.

WATERMELON COOLER - Blended midori, vodka, orange juice and grenadine.

Desserts

APPLE FRITTERS - Chunks of apple lightly battered and fried; sprinkled with cinnamon and sugar.

APPLES BIGNET - Apple rings dipped in a special batter and deep fried; coated with cinnamon sugar, two scoops of ice cream and crushed walnuts.

APRICOT BREAD PUDDING - Warm apricot pudding with rum cashew creme sauce and boysenberry syrup.

BAILEYS CHEESECAKE - Cheesecake with a creamy Bailey's Liquor topping.

BANANA FANTASY - Chocolate-covered bananas with coconut gelato, caramel, pineapple, strawberries and roasted almonds.

BANANA TORTE - A moist and flavorful spice cake layered with Bavarian banana crème and chocolate genache.

BITTERSWEET FLOURLESS CHOCOLATE CAKE - Caramel and chocolate sauce, praline ice cream cone.

BLACK RASPBERRY CHEESECAKE - Made with real black raspberries; a creamy, fluffy texture with a graham cracker crust and a drizzle of black raspberry sauce.

BROWNIE PIE SUPREME - A fresh-baked brownie pie smothered in vanilla ice cream, whipped cream, chocolate syrup and finished with a maraschino cherry.

CARAMEL APPLE PIE - Hand-rolled, buttery crust surrounds a tart Granny Smith apple filling; topped with a generous amount of warm caramel sauce.

CARAMEL FLAN - Vanilla custard, caramel sauce and fresh fruit.

CHARLOTTE AUX FRUITS ROUGES - Ladyfinger marinated in rum and filled with raspberry mousse.

CHILLED APRICOT AND MOSCATO D'ASTI SOUP - Basil ice cream and crispy phyllo triangle.

CHILLED FRUIT SALAD - Oranges, strawberries, rhubarb, kumquat and candied fennel; served with marscapone sorbet and a crisp cookie.

CHOCOLATE ALMOND MIDNIGHT - Dense chocolate mousse cake with maple-almond pralines and raspberry coulis.

CHOCOLATE ALMOND SOUFFLE TORTE - With fresh raspberry coulis.

CHOCOLATE CHERRY DELIGHT - Moist, warm chocolate cake with almond cherry filling, balsamic cherry sauce, almond sorbet and peppered espresso cookie.

CHOCOLATE PRALINE CHEESECAKE - Rich chocolate, crunchy pecans and smooth caramel.

CHOCOLATE SILK PIE - A slice of rich, smooth chocolate that melts in your mouth; made with an Oreo cookie crust and served with a raspberry and mango sauce.

CHOCOLATE VOLCANO - Chunks of brownie, chocolate mousse on a rich brownie tart; topped with chocolate fudge and white chocolate peaks.

CHOCOLATE WALNUT TART - Chocolate walnut tart, creme anglais, chocolate sauce, banana nut ice cream and whipped cream.

COCONUT LIME SORBET - Coconut lime sorbet, tropical fruit and Myers rum.

CRÈME BRÛLÉE - Vanilla custard topped with caramelized brown sugar.

DEATH BY CHOCOLATE - A rich chocolate cake with layers of dark chocolate frosting.

ENGLISH TRIFLE - Layers of rum- and brandy-soaked cake with English custard, strawberries, chantilly cream and toasted almonds.

FIG IN A PASTRY - Blueberry-stuffed fig in crisp pastry dough topped with sauces of nectarine and fig-saba.

FLOURLESS CHOCOLATE CAKE - Served with espresso ice cream, chocolate sauce and fresh berries.

GANÂCHE - Chocolate torte with raspberry purée.

GLACE A LA VANILLE DE GLACE A LA VANILLE DE MADAGASCAR - Madagascar vanilla ice cream with chocolate sauce.

GRANNY SMITH APPLE TARTE - Fresh caramelized cinnamon apples with a white chocolate cream cheese filling in a hazelnut crust; topped with hot caramel sauce.

GULAB JAMUN - Prepared from milk solids soaked in honey.

HOT KEANAKOLU APPLE CRISP - With macadamia nut crumb topping.

KARA KARA FLORENTINE - Oat chocolate wafer, Kara Kara Mandarin sorbet.

KEY LIME PIE WITH MANGO-PAPAYA COULIS - Made with real lime juice; baked in a graham cracker crust.

LAVENDER ICE CREAM - Lavender ice cream, spiced red wine sauce, fresh fruit and whipped cream.

LEMON POUND SHORTCAKE - With confiture of strawberries, whipped cream and strawberry coulis.

LEMON SORBETTO OR VANILLA BEAN ICE CREAM - With raspberry coulis or dark chocolate sauce.

MANGO CRÉME BRÛLÉE - With caramelized sugar, ginger and whipped cream.

MEXICAN CHOCOLATE ICE CREAM - Chocolate and cinnamon ice cream, creme anglais, cinnamon crisps, fresh fruit and whipped cream.

MUD PIE - Chocolate dessert made with chocolate ice cream, flavored with Kahlua, brandy and Tia Maria in an Oreo cookie crust; topped with fudge.

NAPOLÉON AU FRUIT DE LA PASSION - Passion fruit mousse and chocolate napoleon.

PEACH TART - Coconut tart crust and fresh peaches with a coconut crunch sorbet; topped by raspberry syrup.

PINEAPPLE BOYSENBERRY TIMBALE - Pineapple-boysenberry sorbet with raw honey and dried mango hemp seed cream.

PISTA BADAM KHEER - Rice pudding with cardamom and nuts.

PLUM GRANITA - Plum granita and fresh nectarines.

PROFITEROLES - Pastry puffs filled with coffee ice cream, creme anglais, chocolate sauce and whipped cream.

PROFITEROLES AU CHOCOLATE - Petite pastries filled with Häagen Daz vanilla Swiss almond ice cream topped with hot Belgian chocolate and chantilly cream.

RASPBERRY MARTINI - Raspberry sorbet laced with champagne.

STRAWBERRIES ROMANOFF - Fresh strawberries covered with melted ice cream, cinnamon and almonds.

STRAWBERRY RHUBARB SHORTCAKE - Glazed shortcake with strawberry-rhubarb compote and white chocolate mousse topped with mint syrup.

TARTE AU CITRON - Lemon pie, raspberry coulis and creme anglaise.

TIRAMISU - The classic Italian dessert of ladyfingers soaked in espresso, layered with sweet mascarpone cheese and dusted with cocoa powder.

VANILLA TAPIOCA CUSTARD - Marinated cherries, honey almond tuiles and mint syrup.

WHITE AND DARK TRUFFLE - Rich white truffle and dark chocolate mousse with a whisper of whiskey, rests on a light sponge cake; draped in a sheet of dark chocolate.

WHITE CHOCOLATE AMARETTO - The taste of amaretto with loads of almonds wrapped in white chocolate cheesecake.

INDEX

If you enjoyed this book, order the entire series!

1-800-541-1336 Call toll-free
24 hours a day, 7 days a week.
Or fax completed form to:
1-352-622-5836 Order online!
Just go to **www.atlantic-pub.com**
for fast, easy, secure ordering.

Qty	Order Code	Book Title	Price	Total
	Item # RMH-02	THE RESTAURANT MANAGER'S HANDBOOK	$79.95	
	Item # FS1-01	Restaurant Site Location	$19.95	
	Item # FS2-01	Buying and Selling A Restaurant Business	$19.95	
	Item # FS3-01	Restaurant Marketing and Advertising	$19.95	
	Item # FS4-01	Restaurant Promotion and Publicity	$19.95	
	Item # FS5-01	Controlling Operating Costs	$19.95	
	Item # FS6-01	Controlling Food Costs	$19.95	
	Item # FS7-01	Controlling Labor Costs	$19.95	
	Item # FS8-01	Controlling Liquor, Wine and Beverage Costs	$19.95	
	Item # FS9-01	Building Restaurant Profits	$19.95	
	Item # FS10-01	Waiter and Waitress Training	$19.95	
	Item # FS11-01	Bar and Beverage Operation	$19.95	
	Item # FS12-01	Successful Catering	$19.95	
	Item # FS13-01	Food Service Menus	$19.95	
	Item # FS14-01	Restaurant Design	$19.95	
	Item # FS15-01	Increasing Restaurant Sales	$19.95	
	Item # FSALL-01	**Entire 15-Book Series**	**$199.95**	

Best Deal! SAVE 33%
All 15 books for $199.95

Subtotal	
Shipping and Handling	
Florida 6% Sales Tax	
TOTAL	

SHIP TO:

Name_____Phone(____)_____

Company Name_____

Mailing Address_____

City_____State_____Zip_____

FAX_____E-mail_____

❑ My check or money order is enclosed   ❑ Please send my order COD   ❑ My authorized purchase order is attached
❑ Please charge my: ❑ Mastercard ❑ VISA   ❑ American Express ❑ Discover
Card # ☐☐☐☐-☐☐☐☐-☐☐☐☐-☐☐☐☐ Expires ☐☐☐☐

Please make checks payable to: **Atlantic Publishing Company** • 1210 SW 23rd Place • Ocala, FL 34474-7014
USPS Shipping/Handling: add $5.00 first item, and $2.50 each additional or $15.00 for the whole set.
Florida residents PLEASE add the appropriate sales tax for your county.